PRAISE FOR
PRAYER PARTNERS

Years ago, God gave me an assignment to teach on and emphasize prayer. This coincided with what has turned out to be a renewed emphasis on prayer worldwide. During that time, God gave me the idea for the book *Prayer Shield*. After it was written, Elmer Towns told me, "This is the greatest book you have ever written because no one has written on the topic of how leaders can find prayer partners to support their ministry." Everywhere I go, people tell me they have read *Prayer Shield* because Elmer Towns recommended it.

And now, I recommend *Prayer Partners* to you because it will take your prayer ministry to a higher level. The great thing about Elmer's book is that he doesn't just teach you to pray *for* people; he gives great insight into how you can pray *with* people. May God bless both of our books for the advancement of the Kingdom.

DR. C. PETER WAGNER
CHANCELLOR, WAGNER LEADERSHIP INSTITUTE

One of the most gratifying books I've ever written is *Partners in Prayer*, because I know that when people pray for leaders, more will be done for God than ever before. My passion is to train leaders for the Church of Jesus Christ. But more than training leaders, I know that prayer partners for leaders are imperative for the Church today.

I also have a great passion for prayer partners who pray for people other than their leaders. My good friend Elmer Towns has taken this topic to a higher level. He has taught us how to pray *with* people. I'm delighted to envision the contribution Elmer's book *Prayer Partners* will make in the lives of the people of God. My desire is that both of these books will produce more effective prayer in His kingdom.

JOHN MAXWELL
FOUNDER, THE INJOY GROUP

Although men are moved to action by great messages, God is moved to action by humble prayers. The latter statement is the message of this book by Elmer Towns: Prayer will open the floodgates of God's blessing. The foundation of any great ministry is not just found in fiery pulpits; it is found in the sweet savor of the prayer closet. Before we reach the world for Christ, we must first reach the throne of God. And without a doubt, the prayers of the godly alter the course of nations.

DAVID BENOIT
EVANGELIST
PLANO, TEXAS

There is power in agreement. Using sound scriptural principles with great skill, Dr. Towns provides inspiring insights on how God's people can use agreement to release the power of the Holy Spirit in a special way into their lives and the lives of others. These principles are biblical and revolutionary.

BILL BRIGHT
CAMPUS CRUSADE FOR CHRIST

There are many ways to pray. This helpful book emphasizes the powerful benefits of two people agreeing in prayer for anything they ask. I heartily recommend this book that will encourage pastors as well as laity to experience a new dimension in their prayer lives.

DAVID YONGGI CHO
SENIOR PASTOR, YOIDO FULL GOSPEL CHURCH
SEOUL, KOREA

Tapping the power of two—me and you—allows us to experience united divine influence. What a privilege! What a prayer force!

PATSY CLAIRMONT
AUTHOR, *MENDING YOUR HEART IN A BROKEN WORLD*

Like all of Elmer Towns's books, *Prayer Partners* is intensely practical, highly readable, wonderfully spiritual, very transferable, thoroughly biblical and, therefore, unusually powerful. I want to practice and teach it.

DAVE EARLEY
SENIOR PASTOR, NEW LIFE COMMUNITY BAPTIST CHURCH
GAHANNA, OHIO

If you had the opportunity to sit and talk with Dr. Elmer Towns about prayer, you would learn a lot from him. Some of the choicest insights he would share with you are included in this book *Prayer Partners*. When you practice its principles with a family member or friend, I'm confident your prayer life will become a lot more interesting. Even more important, your experience of God's power will be multiplied. Don't miss this fresh presentation of the timeless truths of Scripture—truths that will change you and your world for Christ's glory.

FRANKLIN GRAHAM
PRESIDENT AND CEO
SAMARITAN'S PURSE
BILLY GRAHAM EVANGELISTIC ASSOCIATION

Elmer Towns presents thought-provoking suggestions to be considered by all believers. To those new in the faith and who desire communion with God on a higher plane, he offers insights that will be cherished throughout their spiritual pilgrimage on planet Earth. For the person who has known something of the sweet smell of incense that emanates from the altar of prayer, his remarks will provoke a strong "amen" of agreement.

GLADWIN G. KREIMANN, SR.
SENIOR PASTOR, NORTH ATLANTA BIBLE CHURCH
ATLANTA, GEORGIA

PRAYER PARTNERS

ELMER L. TOWNS

Regal

From Gospel Light
Ventura, California, U.S.A.

Published by Regal Books
From Gospel Light
Ventura, California, U.S.A.
Printed in the U.S.A.

Regal Books is a ministry of Gospel Light, an evangelical Christian publisher dedicated to serving the local church. We believe God's vision for Gospel Light is to provide church leaders with biblical, user-friendly materials that will help them evangelize, disciple and minister to children, youth and families.

It is our prayer that this Regal book will help you discover biblical truth for your own life and help you meet the needs of others. May God richly bless you.

For a free catalog of resources from Regal Books/Gospel Light, please call your Christian supplier or contact us at 1-800-4-GOSPEL *or* www.regalbooks.com.

Cover and Internal Design by Rob Williams
Edited by Ron Durham and Rose Decaen

Library of Congress Cataloging-in-Publication Data
Towns, Elmer L.
    The power of prayer partners / Elmer L. Towns.
        p. cm.
    ISBN 0-8307-2934-8
    1. Prayer groups. I. Title.
    BV287 .T69 2002
    248.3'2—dc21

1 2 3 4 5 6 7 8 9 10 11 12 13 14 15 / 09 08 07 06 05 04 03 02

Rights for publishing this book in other languages are contracted by Gospel Light Worldwide, the international nonprofit ministry of Gospel Light. Gospel Light Worldwide also provides publishing and technical assistance to international publishers dedicated to producing Sunday School and Vacation Bible School curricula and books in the languages of the world. For additional information, visit www.gospellightworldwide.org; write to Gospel Light Worldwide, P.O. Box 3875, Ventura, CA 93006; or send an e-mail to info@gospellightworldwide.org.

CONTENTS

Two-Pray: Taking Prayer to a Higher Level
Have you ever prayed for others with little result?
Two-pray, and these new angles of vision will lift your
intercession to a higher level.

The Power of *Two-Pray*
How partnering in prayer taps into the power of God
and results in blessing others.

Two-Pray Is *Agreement-Praying*
Jesus promises to answer prayer "when two of you agree."
But how much agreement is required?

When You *Warfare-Pray* Against the Enemy
The enemy prevailed against God's people until
prayer partners held up Moses' arms!

When You *Worship-Pray* Effectively
The two angels on the Ark of the Covenant symbolize
how God dwells in the midst of people who agree
in worship and prayer.

When You *Faith-Pray* Together for Ministry
Your ministry will flourish when you learn to pray
together with your fellow workers.

ACKNOWLEDGMENTS

My first and foremost appreciation goes to my wife, Ruth, who has been my prayer partner for 40 years.

Thanks to those who prayed with me early every Sunday morning at my church: Buddy Bryant, Katie Bowles, Donald May, Steve and Shirley Jones, Gladys Rudder, Pat Sheehan, Jerry Cordle and Jack and Mary Clarke.

Thanks to those who pray with me every Wednesday evening: Katherine Thomas, Randall Dill, Chris Liedtke, Harry and Janet Coric, Curtis and Virginia Mays and C. E. Mays. Thank you to Dave Earley, a special prayer partner in 2000-2001.

Thanks to Jerry Falwell for teaching me about how to *faith-pray*. For over 20 years we sat together on our church's platform during prayer meetings. And each week, when the congregation went to prayer, we knelt to *two-pray*.

Thanks to C. Peter Wagner, my good friend of 25 years, who first introduced me to the idea of prayer partners, and to John Maxwell, who organized over 150 men to be his prayer partners at Skyline Wesleyan Church, Greater San Diego, California. Thanks to Bill Klassen who personified a pastoral prayer partner as he supported John Maxwell.

Thanks to my editorial assistant, Linda Elliott, who worked diligently with this manuscript to make it better than what I wrote. Thanks to Renee Grooms, my administrative assistant, who typed the original Bible lessons for the Pastor's Bible Class from which this book was written.

Thanks to Matt Chittum, my graduate assistant, who guided my research over the Internet, and to Jill Walker and Maria Childress, who helped with transcription of the original text.

Thanks to Dr. John Borek, president of Liberty University, who supports my writing ministry. Thanks to Dr. Jim Stevens, associate dean of the School of Religion at Liberty University, who is beginning his twentieth year with me. I could not have written this book if he had not looked after the day-to-day details.

FOREWORD

There are some things we know to be true because throughout a whole lifetime they have proven to be true. As I approach my 80th birthday, one thing I know unequivocally is that the teachings in Elmer Towns's book are true. I know it because this book contains the secret that has opened up every continent of the world to my prayer ministry. It is the secret that has undergirded me with physical strength when there was none in my body. It has called down God's powerful movement in ministry. And, amazingly, this secret has resulted in an exchange of my finite limitations for so much of God's promised infinite power.

Yes, the secret I speak of is people praying together. It works! I know!

Since 1964, I have not even taught a Sunday School class without someone praying for me. I have not ventured overseas unless the 1,000-member 24-hour prayer clock was activated—each intercessor taking a segment of the day or night. I have never written a book, traveled to a seminar or run a committee meeting without my prayer board praying for me on a daily basis through using a telephone prayer chain, and praying *with* me on a monthly basis.

Like Joshua, I have experienced awesome results from my solitary prayers; but I have also found the added comfort, support and love of those who have faithfully and persistently prayed with me. These pray-ers have held up my hands, like Moses' two friends held up his (see Exod. 17:12).

Yes, Dr. Towns's book is a reassuring confirmation of what God has already taught me throughout a lifetime.

But I was also thrilled to discover new varieties and methods of prayer to further enrich my prayer life.

I have known Dr. Elmer Towns for many years. Together, we have confronted Satan in battles over souls still captive in his kingdom—family members, work and school acquaintances, friends and neighbors. Together, we have wept with Jesus as He interceded over sinning Christians and those still spiritually lost on planet Earth. In one accord, we have pleaded for the Holy Spirit to come in His Pentecostal power over our meetings. Whether in the presence of just a few or of thousands, we have prayed, confessing sins that were hindering our relationship with God and His answering our prayers.

God truly does inhabit the place where we consistently pray together. And we have been surprised many times when a stranger or visitor has stepped into that holy place and remarked, "Oh, I can *feel* God here!" "Where two or three are gathered together in My name, I am there in the midst of them" (Matt. 18:20) has been our almost overwhelming experience at times.

Since the mid-1970s, my advisory and prayer board has lived in the third part of God's declaration to Jeremiah: "Call to Me, and I will answer you, and show you great and mighty things, which you do not know" (Jer. 33:3). Praying together does indeed produce overwhelming answers, but it is the unexpected results we didn't even know to pray for that have kept us constantly praising God. The reason is not only because people pray but also because the omnipotent God of heaven hears *and answers* our prayers.

When I was asked to write the curriculum for the AD2000 International Women's Track during the decade of the '90s, I included the simple triplet praying method. This is a prayer method that entails three Christians each choosing the names of three non-Christians and then getting together for a minimum of 15 minutes a week to pray for the salvation of those nine people. The triplet method has proven powerful beyond all expectations as people of all races, cultures, social status and education have gathered to pray for the lost and then to share Jesus with them.

No matter how young or old you are, God is waiting for you to step out in faith and experience a new and deeper relationship with Him—and with your family, church, neighborhood, place of work and/or school. Are you ready, even anxiously waiting, to experience the excitement and thrill of a new level of prayer? Then this book is for you! Or perhaps you don't know there is more in prayer for you? Then this book is especially for you!

Dr. Towns has received deep spiritual insight into the subject of praying together. His book will teach you exciting new prayer principles, and you will also find yourself drawing near to an incredible intimate communion with God—and the people with whom you pray.

If you follow the simple and clear biblical directions in this book—based solidly upon the Bible's old, unchanging principles of prayer—then you are in for the spiritual joyride of your life! Try it and see the amazing things God will do!

Evelyn Christenson
Author, *What Happens When Women Pray*

INTRODUCTION

I accidentally stumbled onto the secret of *two-pray* as I was teaching the Pastor's Bible Class at Thomas Road Baptist Church in 1986. I began praying *with* members of my class, rather than just praying *for* them; and that had a profound influence on both the class members and me. I had such a large class (attendance averaged approximately 1,000) that I didn't know how to keep up with that many people. A large class meeting in the church auditorium has a large number of absentees, so it was easy for people to fall between the cracks and be lost to the church. So I divided the auditorium into sections and placed section leaders over people who sit in the same section. Each week these section leaders were responsible for greeting each person in their section, shaking hands with each member and phoning any absentees in their section to encourage them to return.

Because I don't ask others to do what I myself am unwilling to do, each week I made 5 to 10 absentee phone calls, too. When I phoned people, I ended up praying for them. And it was during one of these phone calls that I unknowingly stumbled on to the power of *two-pray*.

My phone conversations usually began with something like, "Hello, this is Dr. Towns calling from class." Usually the class members greeted me in return, most of the time with surprise that I would take the initiative to phone them. I never asked them why they were absent, because I suspected that such a question would make them feel guilty. It's none of my business why they were not in class. Church attendance is between a person and God.

Then I would say, "I missed you last Sunday, and in a large class it's very easy for people to fall between the cracks." I assured them of my love and concern for them; then I asked, "How may I pray for you?"

The first time I asked "How may I pray for you?" it was an innocent question, intended only to show concern for them. Little did I know that the question would open up great opportunities for pastoral ministries. When I asked, "How may I pray for you?" class members began opening up and sharing their deepest problems. They told me about sicknesses in their family. They told me they were being laid off from their job, their wife left them, or their husband beat them, or their husband was in jail or their children had run away from home. When I asked if I could pray for them, I discovered the incredible number of problems among the people in my class—as well as the very real need they had for prayer.

My response was not to put them off with the promise "I'll pray for you," but to say "Let's pray about it now, over the phone." However, before I prayed about any situation, I would ask another question: "What do you want God to do about this?" Little did I realize at the time what my second question was doing—it allowed the other person to agree with me for an answer.

I discovered that what I wanted God to do was not always the same thing as what they wanted. Once, a middle-aged woman told me that her elderly mother was so ill that she was near death. Obviously, I indicated that I would ask God that her mother be healed.

"Oh, no!" the daughter replied quickly. "She's too far gone—her body organs are not functioning." The daughter wanted to pray that her mother might die without pain. Would it be right for me to ask God to heal an aged mother when the family wants her to die without pain? Obviously we were not in agreement on this prayer.

When I found out what my students wanted God to do, we could *agree-pray*.

Before I prayed I always asked, "After I pray, do you want to pray, too?" Remember, this was a telephone conversation. I didn't want to end my prayer and then have an embarrassing silence over the phone. Some people are reluctant to pray over the phone, while others are reluctant to pray aloud. I found that more than half of the people in the class asked if I would pray aloud myself. Usually they would say something like, "I'll join with you in my heart as you pray." Whether they prayed aloud or not, I felt we were agreeing together on the request.

TWO-PRAY IS BIBLICAL

After I began praying for other people, I then studied the Bible to discover the biblical basis for praying with other people. I discovered a scriptural command: If two of you who pray together will agree on Earth about the request for which you ask, it will be done for them by the Father who is in heaven (see Matt. 18:19).

This promise tells you that your prayers will be answered if you do two things. First, you must agree with your prayer partners about the request before you ask. Second, you must ask together. That's all! If you will do these two things, you will become much more successful in praying. The key is agreeing together.

God answers prayer when you *agree-pray* with another person. Why does He promise to answer prayers when two people agree? We understand why God wants us to separate from sin before He will answer us and why He requires us to draw close to Him in fellowship. But why does He want us to agree with others to get answers?

Because it enhances *harmony, responsibility, accountability* and *productivity* in prayer.

God wants our hearts to be going in the same direction when we pray. Certainly He wants more than *word* agreement. Two people reading the same written prayer is not *agree-pray*. They can say the same words, but their hearts may be going in different directions. Since the word "agree" comes from "harmony" in the original Greek, we know that God is pleased when two people *harmony-pray*.

But why does God like us to harmonize in prayer? Because we become responsible to one another. We each search our heart in the presence of our partner to make sure there are no hindrances. We each strive to get as close to God as possible, and each picks up the passion and sincerity of the other.

And because responsibility leads to accountability in prayer, we each realize that the other person is examining us, just as God examines us. So to speak, we are "eavesdropping" on each other's conversation with God, if not actually joining in with each other's prayers. We become one in spirit as we agree in prayer.

Then, just as accountability leads to productivity in the business world, so in the spiritual world God answers our prayers when He sees that we are as one heart before God. The harmony of *two-pray* leads to

Responsibility—we pray better.
Accountability—we pray honestly.
Productivity—we pray biblically.

NEW EXPRESSIONS OF AN OLD METHOD

Within the method of *two-pray*, there are many expressions. In this book you will find these expressions described by various terms to emphasize their distinguishing features.

For example, when two people *worship-pray*, they are praising God. When they *fellowship-pray*, they are enjoying His presence. When they *intercede-pray*, they focus on the needs of another. When they *warfare-pray*, they are wrestling with the enemy as they seek spiritual protection. And *faith-pray* is when they know they will receive an answer before it comes.

Two-pray is a method of prayer, not a type. Nor is it the solution to all unanswered prayer. It is simply a manner of praying that involves two people joining together to approach the Father in prayer.

We can apply the method of *two-pray* to the old adage "Methods are many, principles are few; methods may change, but principles never do."

This is true of prayer. There are only a few principles of prayer, and they never change. And because these principles are eternal, they must be followed if we expect God to answer our prayers. We must pray sincerely . . . pray in fellowship with God . . . pray in believing faith . . . pray continuously . . . pray separated from sin . . . pray according to Scripture . . . and pray to the glory of God.

The above adage also means there can be many methods to approach the Father. *"Two-pray"* is only a new term for an old method. Although Christians have always prayed together, the phrase *"two-pray"* can help us focus anew on this method. Of course there are other methods of prayer as well. We can pray in secret, with a small group, in a large group, through the words of a hymn or through the Lord's Prayer. When you *two-pray* with a friend, you are simply using one of the many methods of prayer.

The method of *two-pray* opens up many other expressions of prayer. When two agree to intercede for a great project, they *vision-pray*. When two agree on what they desire for God to do, they *faith-pray*. When two are waiting for God's direction, they *listen-pray*. When one is confident but the other is not, they *support-pray*. When two just enjoy God, they *fellowship-pray*. When two sing their request, they *hymn-pray*. When two especially feel the presence of Jesus, they *Jesus-pray*. And when two experience the Holy Spirit, they *Spirit-pray*.

This is not a comprehensive list. You will find other expressions of prayer explained in this book. Try all of them, not for fun or excitement or novelty, but to draw closer to God and to realize answers to your prayers. Consider these new prayer terms as ways to gain new insights into old truths. They have always been available to God's people. Many praying saints have used the same ideas and expressions without using the new terms.

So why have I invented new and special names? I wanted to ana-lyze the various ways to pray and the conditions under which we pray and then put them in a new package to help you understand their importance. The business world does this all the time. Take the example of shoe polish.

Before I was born, my daddy bought shoe polish for a penny. When I was a boy, I would buy polish for a nickel. It came in a small tin can that was hard to open. You would use an old rag to apply the polish to your shoes, a brush to make them shine and, finally, a special cloth to get a spit polish on the shoes. Today, shoe polish can be purchased in a large plastic package with an applicator built into the top. You don't need brushes and shine rags—one application does it all.

This book is a new package of old ways of praying. I have broken down the various aspects of prayer into new terms to make it easier to understand, because intercessory prayer is never easy. It is the hardest thing in the world to wrestle with vicious demon forces. You are standing between light and darkness.

My pastor constantly quotes Ecclesiastes 1:9, "There is nothing new under the sun." That means my new terms for prayer are not new concepts. They are the old Bible ways to pray with a new title or handle (remember when a name was called a handle?), i.e., something to help you get a better grip on prayer.

I am encouraging you to get a grip on how to pray in new ways—not new to God but to you. I challenge you to approach God on your knees with new attitudes. *Faith-pray* with a new boldness; *Jesus-pray* with a new assurance; *Spirit-pray* with a new purpose; *worship-pray* with new reverence.

I want you to be able to measure your results from *ask-pray*, to give strength to your prayer partner in *support-pray* and to learn from each other by *insight-pray*. I want you to become more consistent in *discipline-pray* and to intercede for specific projects in *vision-pray*.

I want you to understand that prayer is a process that leads us to God, so that you will *continue-pray* and not give up too soon. I want you to intercede for lost people with *outreach-pray* and *evangelistic-pray*.

If you don't have a prayer partner, then follow the suggestions of chapter 9 on how to find someone, so you can *two-pray*. When you use all these expressions of prayer with a friend, you both will grow in grace and in the ministry of outreach.

No matter what you call it, no matter how you do it, no matter who you do it with; whatever you do, *pray*; prayer is the essential act of talking to God. He needs to hear from you, and you need to hear from Him. So do it now!

ELMER TOWNS
Written from my home at the foot of the
Blue Ridge Mountains of Virginia
Spring 2001

THE POWER OF
Two-Pray

In the adult Sunday School class that I lead, we begin with a song service that lasts about 30 minutes. During that half hour, I walk around greeting people, and as I do so, many of them stop me to ask for prayer.

On the morning I wrote this chapter, a lady told me she was having chemotherapy the next morning; she stood, and we clasped hands together and prayed while the congregation was singing.

Then a couple stopped to tell me they were going to court to request legal custody of their granddaughter, whose father, their son-in-law, didn't want his daughter in a Christian school or church. But this couple felt it was important for them to keep a Christian influence on their granddaughter. The three of us stood and held hands as we prayed.

Another lady whom I had led to the Lord 14 years before told me that she was having cataract surgery that week. Because she couldn't stand, I knelt beside her as she sat in the pew, and we prayed.

I use these illustrations to suggest that *two-pray* is so powerful that God hears our prayer any time, any place, under any condition. Not only does a supernaturally powerful God work wonders in *two-pray*, but there is also power in one Christian's taking the time just to pray for another. I've been told "Your prayers gave me strength to face an operation," and "I gained the strength to deal with my husband's affair because of your prayer." Others have said they grew in hope or love just because they knew someone was concerned enough about them to pray with them and for them.

WHAT *TWO-PRAY* CAN DO
FOR OTHERS

Both Scripture and experience show us the power of *two-pray*.

You Can Help Deliver People from Trouble
"Man who is born of woman is of few days and full of trouble" (Job 14:1). But when you pray about the troubles of others, you can help deliver them from danger or problems. In the very early days of the Church, King Herod killed the apostle James before the believers could intervene with a prayer movement to save his life. But when Herod put Peter in prison, massive prayer was launched, and the Lord delivered him from prison (see Acts 12:1-5,17). You can come alongside those in trouble to pray for them so that God delivers them.

You Can Move God to Heal Someone
No one can understand the mind or purpose of God, why He heals one person and allows another to die. Believers trust that ours is a loving God who has "mercy on whom He wills" (Rom. 9:18). Because you don't know the will of God, you should pray equally for all people to be healed. You are commanded to "pray for one another, that you may be healed" (Jas. 5:16). God would not tell us to pray for physical healing if He did not intend to heal.

You Can Help Others Live Peacefully
Paul said, "I urge . . . that requests, prayers, intercession and thanksgiving be made for everyone . . . that we may live peaceful and quiet lives in all godliness and holiness" (1 Tim. 2:1, *NIV*). *Two-pray* is an

excellent opportunity to ask God that others have the good life—a godly life, a holy life.

You Can Help Protect Others from Temptation

Remember how Jesus prayed for Simon Peter when Satan sought him (see Luke 22:31-32). Since Jesus is our example, and since we are taught to pray "Lead us not into temptation," we can also pray that others will be protected from temptation. I often pray for our children and grandchildren, as well as those Christians who are under our ministry.

You Can Pray for the Ministry of Others

Do you have friends who are Sunday School teachers, pastors or others who serve the Lord in different ways? You can *two-pray* for their successful ministry (see also chapter 9). That is why Paul asked the Christians in Rome to "join me in my struggle by praying to God for me" (Rom. 15:30, *NIV*). He asked the believers in Colossae to pray "that God may open a door for our message" (Col. 4:3, *NIV*).

You Can Help Others Understand and Grow

If you are a Christian leader, you want those who listen to you to have spiritual understanding. If you are a parent, you want your children to grow in spiritual knowledge. You can pray for these people as Paul prayed for the Ephesians: "I keep asking that . . . the glorious Father, may give you the Spirit of wisdom and revelation, so that you may know him better" (Eph. 1:17, *NIV*). You can contribute to the spiritual growth of others, praying, like Paul, that they will be strengthened "with power through his Spirit in your inner being, so that Christ may dwell in your hearts through faith" (Eph. 3:16-17, *NIV*).

THE SOURCE OF *TWO-PRAY'S* POWER

There are some important reasons for the power of *two-pray*, both in the lives of those we pray for and in the lives of the pray-ers themselves.

You Tap into the Power of the Word

We have noticed that Jesus told Peter, "I have prayed for you, Simon, that your faith may not fail" (Luke 22:32, *NIV*). We have seen that Paul was a regular intercessor for the churches he established. We have seen that the Early Church prayed and secured the release of Peter when he was arrested.

Why is it important to follow these examples? Because they are in the Word of God, which means that they share in the power that created the worlds (see John 1:1-3). When you follow examples in the Word, you tap into its power.

You Are Obeying a Scriptural Command

When Paul wrote to young Timothy, he did more than give an example of *two-pray*; he gave a scriptural command that "requests, prayers, intercession and thanksgiving be made for everyone" (1 Tim. 2:1, *NIV*). This is also your command and commission to be an intercessor for others. Obedience to God's commands is not a work of salvation, but it is direct evidence of salvation (see Eph. 2:8-10).

You Fulfill Your Responsibility

You have many responsibilities to the unsaved and to other believers. One of those duties is to pray for them. James said, "Pray for one another" (Jas. 5:16). Are you fulfilling this responsibility?

You Express Your Love for Others

When Jesus was asked which is the first great commandment in the Law, He answered, "'You shall love the LORD your God with all your heart, with all your soul, and with all your mind.' And the second is like it: 'You shall love your neighbor as yourself'" (Matt. 22:37,39). After love for God, you are required to love others; and you cannot express your love for anyone in a better way than by praying God's blessing on them.

You Put Your Faith into Action

When you pray for other people by faith, knowing that God is listening to your request, you demonstrate *confident-pray*. When you know God will answer, you *faith-pray*. James reminds us of this confidence: "The prayer of faith will save the sick, and the Lord will raise him up" (Jas. 5:15).

You Bear the Burdens of Others

When you *two-pray*, you actually come alongside others to help them carry their load. "Bear one another's burdens, and so fulfill the law of Christ" (Gal. 6:2). When others are overwhelmed by their troubles, you can help them by praying for their deliverance. But go beyond interceding for them; join them in prayer.

You Carry Out the Great Commission

After Jesus' resurrection, He reminded His followers of the Great Commission, "You shall be witnesses to Me in Jerusalem, and in all Judea and Samaria, and to the end of the earth" (Acts 1:8). Did the disciples begin preaching immediately after they received this command to evangelize the world? No! They returned to Jerusalem and went into the Upper Room, where they "continued with one accord in prayer and supplication" (Acts 1:14). *The first step in carrying out the Great Commission was prayer.* Other references showed that they prayed for God to use them, for power in preaching, for unity among the small circle of believers, and that those who would hear the gospel would become convicted and be converted.

Are you helping to carry out the Great Commission by interceding for the lost?

You Help Deliver Others from Sin

Sometimes other people are so bound in sin that they can't even pray for themselves. Like a python, sin has coiled itself around them to squeeze out their life. People helplessly addicted to sin are usually not able to pray for themselves. Such was the case when Israel sinned in the wilderness. God sent death-serpents among them in judgment. "The people came to Moses, and said, 'We have sinned . . . pray to the LORD that He take away the serpents from us'" (Num. 21:7).

Just as God's Old Testament people were saved by the intercession of Moses, people can be delivered from sin and addiction today by your intercession.

You Grow in the Same Areas
When you pray for the faith of others, God will usually increase your faith. It's the same with love, grace and humility. As you pray for others, God usually gives to you what you ask for them. "Give, and it will be given to you" (Luke 6:38). God has even been known to bring financial relief to those who prayed for the financial needs of others, because they demonstrated an unselfish concern for the needs of others.

WHY DO SO FEW PEOPLE
TWO-PRAY?

In the light of the power of *two-pray*, why is it relatively rare? We are drawn to the Bible accounts of heroes and heroines who stood alone against the world—Noah and his family against an ungodly world, Abraham against the idolaters of his homeland, Joseph in the midst of the paganism in Egypt, Elijah standing alone against 450 prophets of Baal. But in this chapter we have also seen ample evidence of people standing with others in prayer. Why have these examples not been as compelling as the others?

Rugged American Individualism?
Our great country was carved out of the wilderness by the isolated pioneer against great odds, with limited resources, in difficult circumstances. The rugged individualist planted crops, started businesses, sailed ships and defeated his enemies. No wonder many Americans come to the Word of God with a self-perception shaped by this national experience.

Believers, however, must be willing to allow the Bible to reshape their own cultural experience. The Bible is as full of examples of

God's people standing together as it is of rugged heroes standing alone. The apostle Paul was especially concerned that we view the Church as a body with many members working harmoniously, standing together. *Two-pray* is a biblical way to make this picture a reality.

The individual Christian is not like the little Dutch boy who put his finger in the dike to save a nation. You need not feel that you are a David standing against Goliath. For years we have bought self-help books on everything from emotional health to carpentry and even spirituality. Isn't it time now to emphasize the other side of the coin and admit that we could multiply our ministry by partnering with another Christian in prayer?

Not Knowing About *Two-Pray*

Many people don't partner in prayer with others simply because they haven't heard it preached from the pulpit or taught in Bible classes. But in addition to the many Bible examples of *two-pray*, a few voices throughout Christian history can help dispel this ignorance.

Boniface, a Church leader at the beginning of the Middle Ages, was looking for prayer partners as he wrestled the demonic forces of Germany. In the year A.D. 500 he wrote, "We entreated the piety of your brotherliness that we may be helped by your devout petitions . . . that the few seeds scattered in the bushes may spring up and grow."[1] Boniface was looking for prayer partners.

King Mangs II of the Scandinavian Revival in 1700 prayed, "Lord, bless my intercessors today."[2] He had learned to pray for his intercessors before they prayed for him.

In our own times, C. Peter Wagner, when he taught at Fuller Theological Seminary, challenged each student to go out and recruit prayer intercessors. According to Peter, he found that when his intercessors made his ministry their ministry, their ministry grew and his ministry grew.

Examples of partnership prayer in Scripture, in the history of the Church and in modern times are too numerous to use ignorance as an excuse for not *two-praying*.

Reluctance to Be Open with Others

Perhaps you don't have a prayer partner because you don't open up to others easily. *Two-praying* is extremely intimate. You invite your prayer partner into your heart just like you invite a friend into your kitchen or into that secret closet where you keep your linens. You may even be reluctant to open up with someone else because of hidden sin in your life.

TWO-PRAY OR NOT *TWO-PRAY*: THAT IS THE QUESTION

Teaming
With
Others for
Powerful
Results
Allows God to Use
Your Life!

However, all you have to lose by overcoming such fears is your emptiness and isolation. *Two-praying* can begin with the pray-ers themselves, each interceding for the other. You know that God knows your inner thoughts. Why not experience the release of having your life open and aboveboard with another believer, too?

The Problem of Spiritual Pride

Maybe you don't ask others to pray with you because you are like the little child who pushes away the father's hand saying, "I can do it myself!" Even an innocent child can be ignorant—the child does not realize how much he must learn, how much others can help him and how big the problems are in this world. No child can make it alone, and no Christian can make it without the help of another.

Even the great evangelist Dwight L. Moody was guilty of spiritual pride. When two ladies told him, "We are praying for you, Mr. Moody," he replied: "Why don't you pray for the unsaved people . . . not for me." Eventually, however, Moody came to feel an emptiness in his life and ministry; and he lowered his defenses and asked these dedicated women to pray for him.

"We got down on our knees," he wrote. "They poured out their hearts, that I might receive the anointing of the Holy Ghost." And when that anointing occurred, Moody admitted, "I would not be placed back where I was before that blessed experience if you would give me all Glasgow."[3]

The Problem of Unhealthy Humility

Some people feel that they are not worthy of God's blessings and that they do not deserve for anyone to pray for them or with them. All of us would do well to remember that in our sinful nature we *are* totally depraved. We are incapable of doing anything to gain merit before God. There is no reason why God should use any of us, in partnership prayer or any other ministry.

But limiting ourselves to that fact ignores the good news! God sent His Son to die for you. And in the words of the first of the Four Spiritual Laws, "God loves you and has a wonderful plan for your life."[4] You have been commissioned to carry out the Great Commission and to love God with all your heart and your neighbor as yourself. You are absolutely important to God and imperative to His work. You have such a great responsibility that you can't afford false humility. You must realize that God "works in you both to will and to do for His good pleasure" (Phil. 2:13).

YOUR TURN NOW

Now you understand the power of *two-pray*. This doesn't mean that you should forget the importance of partnering with Jesus and the Spirit in personal prayer. Don't forget to *Jesus-pray*; but remember that if you are so in love with Jesus that it just shines through, you may be able to demonstrate that love in *two-pray* with another person. Don't forget to *Spirit-pray*; maybe you know someone who needs to experience the power of the Holy Spirit and could partner with him or her in prayer.

Now you must look for opportunities to pray with others. You must look for a prayer partner. Now your prayer ministry can be transformed by becoming focused on others. Learn to intercede for them, to become concerned for their problems and needs.

TAKE-AWAY PRAYER PRINCIPLES

1. I know about *two-pray*, so I have no excuse for avoiding it.
2. I know the power of *two-pray* from Scripture, and that obedience to the command to pray with and for others taps in to that power.
3. I can *partner-pray* only if I am not too self-reliant and proud.
4. I can have a fruitful ministry if I pray with and for others, and open up my heart to allow them to pray for me.

CHAPTER 2

TWO-PRAY IS
Agreement-Praying

Doug Oldham, the famous gospel singer, earned two gold records for albums that sold a half-million copies, and his album of the musical "Alleluia" sold over a million copies. While he became widely known as a powerful gospel singer in churches during the '70s and '80s, during the '90s he and his wife became famous in heaven for intercessory prayer. The Oldhams are effective examples of *two-pray* intercessors.

Phil Captain, a psychology professor at Liberty University, was diagnosed in December 1996 with a large, cancerous tumor in his abdomen. He entered the hospital at the point of death and was placed in intensive care. Before his surgery, I visited Phil's hospital room to pray for him, and then I left.

But not Doug and Laura Lee Oldham. They had an assignment from God. They spent time with Phil before surgery and with the family during the actual operation. They were not friends of the Captains at the time, but they certainly became friends thereafter. Doug said, "Laura Lee prays to touch God, I pray to rebuke any evil spirits, and on occasion when the demons return, I have had to tell them not to come back." Several times during the five-hour operation, the Oldhams gathered the family into a circle to ask God to heal Phil. Yet the report was bleak after the operation.

Pastor Jerry Falwell announced to the church in a prayer meeting that Phil—apart from divine intervention—would be dead in three weeks. That evening, Jerry and I knelt on the platform as I led us in prayer. "Lord," I prayed, "we need Phil to teach at Liberty University. He is an outstanding Ph.D. in clinical psychology, and he has deep insight into the biblical nature of counseling. The University needs his testimony, and the students need his influence . . . Lord, heal him."

Then Jerry Falwell began his prayer. "Lord, I agree with Elmer; heal Phil and bring him back to us." This is another illustration of *two-pray*.

After I heard the confident voice of Falwell in his *faith-pray*, I saw a glimmer of hope and gained the courage to believe that God might possibly heal Phil. Three weeks passed, and Phil did not die. He also believed in the power of the prayers being offered for his healing.

Two weeks later, however, the tumor returned, and Phil had to endure five months of chemotherapy. In the dark moments, Phil's faith never wavered. And we kept praying.

Doug Oldham got up early, about 5 A.M., and stopped by the hospital each morning to lay hands on Phil and to pray for and with him. Although he said he did not anoint with oil at the beginning of his ministry, he began to later. He said he doesn't know why God often heals when oil is used, but that he began to use it in faith, simply because God's Word says to (see Jas. 5:14). So Doug and Laura Lee anointed Phil with oil and *faith-prayed* for healing.

"We usually sing when we pray," Doug and Laura Lee told me. "It opens God's arms and creates an atmosphere to heal." So they *hymn-prayed* over Phil, too.

God healed Phil, and there are no signs of physical or mental damage. Soon he was back teaching a full load of classes, and a year after his operation he ran the Virginia 10-Miler race. The surgeon on the case, who is not a believer, said, "I have never used the word 'miracle,' but I think it applies in this case."

CONDITIONS FOR *TWO-PRAY*

What conditions of prayer should we agree upon? When you kneel with your partner in prayer, both of you bring some assumptions to God. Obviously, these assumptions should be biblical.

1. Believe That God Is Able

First, you should agree that God does hear and can answer any prayer. "Is anything too hard for the LORD?" (Gen. 18:14). When two people know the Word of God and believe that its promises are true, you both should believe that God can do anything He promised. And beyond your biblical confidence, you have experienced answers to prayer in the past. So you should both agree that God is able to answer this present request. Just remember the three "ables" of God:

> *Omniscience*: God is able to know all things.
> *Omnipotence*: God is able to do all things.
> *Omnipresence:* God is able to be everywhere present at the same time.

2. Believe That God Will Hear

A step beyond believing that God *can* hear is agreeing with your prayer partner that He *will* hear. *Two-pray* involves agreeing that:

> Behold, the LORD's hand is not shortened, that it cannot save; nor His ear heavy, that it cannot hear. But your iniquities have separated you from your God; and your sins have hidden His face from you, so that He will not hear (Isa. 59:1-2).

3. Believe That God Will Answer

Third, when you agree that God can *heal* and that He will *hear*, prayer partners agree that He will *answer*. This is the prayer of faith spoken of in James 5:15. Of course, it is understood that this is true only when God's conditions for answered prayer have been met.

These conditions can be summarized as follows:

1. Ask sincerely.
2. Ask in faith that you will receive an answer.
3. Continue asking.
4. Ask according to the Scriptures.
5. Ask in Jesus' name.
6. Ask to glorify the Father.
7. Ask according to the will of God.
8. Ask when sins are forgiven.

4. Be Yielded to God's Will

The fourth area of agreement is yieldedness. When both you and your prayer partner are yielded to God, you are agreeing to His conditions as outlined above. At this point the believer and the unbeliever have two different questions:

The unbeliever's question is, *Can* God . . . ?
The Christian's question is, *Will* God . . . ?

5. Prayer's Urgency

You and your prayer partner should agree on the urgency of the request. You are of one mind in believing, "Lord, we need You . . . we need You right away. Unless You intervene, there'll be great tragedy." When you and your partner desperately need an answer from God and the two of you can agree on the urgency, then you can *two-pray* with fervency. When you both agree that God can interrupt the circumstances and reverse the tide that's flowing against you, then you can *faith-pray*.

6. No Other Source

God answers prayer when you and your prayer partner can agree that there is no other alternative at the present, that your back is to the wall, that there is nowhere to turn but to God. The old adage says, "You're between a rock and a hard place."

This was the attitude of the apostle Peter when he asked, "Lord, to whom shall we go?" (John 6:68). He was saying that he could turn to no one but God alone. This is where weeping, begging and fasting become an additional basis for your prayers.

7. Honesty and Openness

You and your prayer partner must be honest and open with each other. Sometimes you can "feel" when the other person is holding back, or you "know" they are not telling you all of the truth. At the same time, sometimes you "absolutely know" when the other person is 100 percent honest. When both of you reach total honesty with one another, then you can agree in your *two-pray* that "it will be done for [you] by My Father in heaven" (Matt. 18:19).

8. Using All Kinds of Prayer

In this eighth area of agreement, you and your partner must examine carefully the Word of God to see all the various ways that people prayed in the Bible. You must agree to *clean-pray*, because "we know that God does not hear sinners" (John 9:31). Of course since "all have sinned" (Rom. 3:23), this does not mean that you are perfect; but it means that you and your prayer partner agree not to deliberately live in sin.

- You must agree to *faith-pray*. "Whatever things you ask in prayer, believing, you will receive" (Matt. 21:22).
- You must agree to *Bible-pray*. "If . . . My words abide in you, you will ask what you desire, and it shall be done for you" (John 15:7).
- You agree to *Jesus-pray*. "If you ask anything in My name, I will do it" (John 14:14).
- You must agree to *search-pray*. "You will . . . find Me, when you search for Me with all your heart" (Jer. 29:13).
- You must agree to *confident-pray*. "He who comes to God must believe that He is, and that He is a rewarder of those who diligently seek Him" (Heb. 11:6).

- You must agree to *marriage harmony-pray*. "Husbands, likewise, dwell with [your wives] with understanding, giving honor to the wife . . . that your prayers may not be hindered" (1 Pet. 3:7).
- And finally, you must agree to *two-pray*. "If two of you agree . . . it will be done" (Matt. 18:19).

9. Really Asking

Two-pray is not a vague wishing that God would do something; it is actually asking God to do something. Prayer partners must agree to actually ask together.

In Matthew 18:19 the Greek word for "ask" is *aiteo*, which is simply to ask, to request, to call for or to petition. Many other words are used as synonyms of prayer—"communion," "fellowship," "worship," "praise," "confession," etc. But when God tells you to ask, then you should do what He tells you to do. Only after you and your prayer partner have actually asked the Father do you activate an answer from Him.

10. Total Commitment

Finally, both you and your prayer partner must totally commit your lives to God, and to the expectation that He will answer your prayer. When two of you agree, you shouldn't pray, "If it be Your will," or "I'd sure like it if You could get around to it." When you a*gree-pray*, there are no loopholes, no alternate plans and no changing your mind.

When a young man asks a girl out for a date but tacks on a condition—"If it doesn't rain," or "If things work out"—that's not a sincere invitation. Sometimes our prayers are not sincere, because we hold back like that. Remember God's promise: "You will seek Me and find Me, when you search for Me with all your heart" (Jer. 29:13).

What Does "Agreement" Mean?

When Jesus tells us that "If two of you agree on earth concerning anything that they ask" (Matt. 18:19), what does He mean by the word "agree"? Actually, Jesus uses the Greek word *sumphoneo*, which gives us our word "symphony."

When you go to the symphony, you first hear the orchestra tuning up. It can be disconcerting, because it's not musical; it's screeching and discordant because every instrument is doing its own thing. You are waiting for the conductor to raise his baton. That is when the instruments come together in harmony. That is what you came to hear.

It's the same thing with prayer. We can pray individually, but we must also learn to pray in harmony—"in symphony"—with others. To pray without agreement is "screeching" in the Lord's ears. We can solve this disharmony by agreeing with others as we pray.

WHY *AGREEMENT-PRAY* IS IMPORTANT

Agreement Reflects the Father and Son

Jesus said, "I and My Father are one" (John 10:30). Since prayer partners pray in Jesus' name, their prayers should reflect the unity between the Father and Son. When we pray together in unity, God is glorified. When we pray at odds with each other, we are painting a false picture of disunity between the Father and Son.

Agreement Answers the Prayer of Our Lord

The night before Jesus died, He prayed for our united fellowship:

> I do not pray for these alone, but also for those who will believe in Me through their word; that they all may be one, as You, Father, are in Me, and I in You; that they also may be one . . . just as We are one (John 17:20-22).

When you agree with your prayer partner and kneel in prayer together, you are fulfilling Jesus' prayer for His followers.

Two-Pray Reflects Agreement on Repentance

When you *two-pray*, it is a visual picture of repentance in action. Why? Because going your own way is straying away from God toward sin—

"All we like sheep have gone astray; we have turned, every one, to his own way" (Isa. 53:6).

The first sin of the devil, Lucifer, was turning away from God to do his own thing. Likewise the world is filled with people doing what is right in their own eyes. When you turn to the Lord for salvation, you stop going your own way. You follow Jesus, who said, "Come to Me" (Matt. 11:28) and "I am the way" (John 14:6). In doing this, you join many other believers who also follow Jesus, becoming a great throng of people testifying that they want to repent of going their own way, and to follow Jesus instead.

Two-Pray Agreement Fulfills Scripture

Paul commanded us to endeavor to "keep the unity of the Spirit in the bond of peace" (Eph. 4:3). When you kneel together in *two-pray* agreement, God is pleased with your obedience, because you are testifying to the "bond of peace" between you. In this way you are positioning yourself so God can answer your request.

Disunity Harms Ministry

Two women were arguing in the church at Philippi. Paul had to write about their disunity, forever telling the readers of the Scriptures that these two women couldn't get along: "I implore Euodia and I implore Syntyche to be of the same mind in the Lord" (Phil. 4:2). No one knows what they were fussing about and today no one cares. Neither do we know what harm they brought to the church because of their bickering, or what they could have accomplished in ministry if they had prayed together.

Disunity Harms Your Prayers

Jesus often reminded us that we need to forgive others before God answers our prayers.

> And whenever you stand praying, if your have anything against anyone, forgive him, that your Father in heaven may also forgive you your trespasses. But if you do not forgive,

neither will your Father in heaven forgive your trespasses (Mark 11:25-26).

In other words, your prayers are useless if you have a broken relationship with another believer. You can't honestly *two-pray* with another if you have ill will toward them or others in your heart.

Disunity Eats Away at Character

Paul identified those qualities that he called "the works of the flesh" which destroy your spirituality. Notice how many of the following italicized sins reflect your disunity with another person:

Now the works of the flesh are evident, which are: adultery, fornication, uncleanness, lewdness, idolatry, sorcery, *hatred, contentions, jealousies, outbursts of wrath, selfish ambitions, dissensions,* heresies, *envy,* murders, drunkenness, revelries, and the like; of which I tell you beforehand, just as I also told you in time past, that those who practice such things will not inherit the kingdom of God (Gal. 5:19-21, emphasis added).

God knows the attitudes and thoughts of your heart. He turns away from listening to your prayers when you harbor sin (see Ps. 66:18; Isa. 59:1-2). But dealing with these sins as you kneel to *two-pray*, you get God's attention.

HOW CLOSE MUST YOUR AGREEMENT BE?

Can people who want to *two-pray* disagree on some things? Obviously, no two people in this world see everything alike. We have gender differences, age differences and racial differences, which means that we may see things differently because we come from different groups. Don't forget geographical differences, IQ differences and personality differences. We differ about theology, church government, church names and different worship expressions to God.

Granted that people are different, what should we agree about when we pray?

When two people kneel to pray, can one be a Methodist who believes in free will and the other a Presbyterian who believes in predestination? To get their prayers answered, must they agree on every point of theology?

AGREEING IN PRAYER IS LIKE TAKING A JOURNEY TOGETHER

—Agree on Destination
—Agree on the Purpose
—Agree on the Road
—Agree on the Speed
—Agree on the Results

When a couple picks out a church to attend, must they agree with the type of music or the type of sermon preached on a regular basis? Some churches sing the historic hymns to remind them of the depths of theology and heritage of our faith. Other churches sing praise music and find their hearts are stirred to worship the Lord Jesus. Two can be from different theological backgrounds, but they can sing in harmony because they agree to follow the music on the page. Just so, two can pray together in harmony because they agree on what they want God to do for them.

When It Is All Right to Disagree

We live in a day when tolerance is expected by liberal media and by non-Christian public perception. We are expected to accept everyone's philosophy and agree with them in all things. But there are certain areas where we Christians disagree with nonbelievers. For example, we can't expect God to hear their prayer (see John 9:31) unless they are open to receiving Christ. That doesn't make us narrow or bigoted. We must be as narrow as Jesus was when He said, "I am the way, the truth, and the life. No one comes to the Father except through Me" (John 14:6).

But there will be times when Christians disagree with each other. Even in their disagreement, however, they must agree on some basics so that what they agree on is more than what they disagree on. What are some of the things you can disagree on yet still kneel with a brother or sister and agree in prayer together?

First, you can disagree on minor points but not major doctrine. If you disagree on the essentials of Christianity or the fundamentals of the faith, you disagree on the essence of faith. When we use the word "essential" to describe what things are absolutely necessary to make a car run, we mean that we can't operate a car without an engine, wheels, steering wheel, etc. There is no use in agreeing to take a trip if you can't agree on what's necessary to make the car run.

The same thing is true with Christianity. Certain doctrines are essential, and certain ones are not. Just as a car can operate without fenders, back seats and a trunk, so can prayer partners *two-pray* in agreement without agreeing on nonessentials such as the mode of baptism, the nature of tongues, church names and how often to take the Lord's Supper.

We don't have to write a creed to discover the essentials of the faith. The apostle Paul himself describes what is "of first importance" in 1 Corinthians 15:3-4 (*NIV*):

For what I received I passed on to you as of first importance:
that Christ died for our sins according to the Scriptures,
that he was buried, that he was raised on the third day
according to the Scriptures.

Since Paul is teaching on the truth of the death, burial and resurrection of Jesus in this passage as recorded in the inspired Scriptures, we can add that to the fundamentals of the faith. When we do that, the following essential doctrines of Christianity emerge:

1. *The inspiration and authority of the Scriptures*—if the Bible is not our authority in faith, then we can be sure of nothing.
2. *The virgin birth and deity of Jesus Christ*—if Jesus is not both God and man, then His life was not sinless and He could not have died for our sins.
3. *The substitutionary death to forgive sins*—if Jesus didn't die for our sins, then we have no basis for forgiveness.
4. *The bodily resurrection of Jesus from the dead*—if Jesus was not raised from the dead, then eternal life is not possible.
5. *The physical return of Jesus to receive believers to Himself*—if Jesus doesn't return for believers, then all the promises of our eternal future in heaven are void and we have no hope.

So you can disagree with your prayer partner on minor nonessentials, but if you disagree with him or her on any of the above essentials of Christianity, your faith won't work because the two of you have denied the essence or fundamentals of Christianity.

Second, you must agree on the clear teaching of the Bible. You can disagree on obscure interpretations of difficult parts of Scripture, but there's an old adage that says "When God hasn't spoken, don't make rules." There are many things in the Bible that are not clear or not mentioned; but since many Christians *think* they are there, they make rules for themselves and others based on what is obscure instead of what is clear.

For example, many people try to prove that their particular form of church government is the only form authorized by the Bible, even though very little is said in Scripture about the way churches should operate. When God whispers, you should not shout. Or to put it another way: "Don't sharpen your pencil point too sharp when it comes to church government . . . if you press your point, you will break it."

It may well be that God was not explicit on church government and many other nonessentials so a variety of different people groups could be incorporated into the one Body despite differences in age, cultures, occupations, gender, etc. If God had made churches as narrow as some people think He did, many groups of people might be excluded from full church membership.

What does this mean to you and your prayer partner? Agree on the things that are obvious, but agree to disagree on obscure points. Then you can still *two-pray* together.

YOUR TURN NOW

Now you understand why *two-pray* is effective. According to Jesus in Matthew 18:19, when you intercede with a partner you are much more likely to get your request answered than when you pray alone. Your prayer partner makes you accountable to the Scriptures and makes you honestly face your own understanding of what you must do. So take your prayers to a higher level by finding a prayer partner and *two-praying* with them.

Now what must you do? "Call to Me, and I will answer you, and show you great and mighty things, which you do not know" (Jer. 33:3).

From this chapter we have discovered these take-away values:

TAKE-AWAY PRAYER PRINCIPLES

1. I can *two-pray* for the healing of those expected to die.
2. I must agree with my prayer partner in spirit and on major issues.
3. I don't have to agree with every aspect of others' lives to effectively *two-pray* with them.
4. I must agree to meet the conditions of prayer with my prayer partner in order to get answers.
5. I must go beyond agreement to *two-pray* in asking the Father to receive the answers we seek.

WHEN YOU
Warfare-Pray
AGAINST THE
ENEMY

Moses stood on the high peak, watching the battle unfold before him on the plain. God's people, Israel, were being attacked by the evil nation of Amalek, which hated Jehovah and any thought of godly purity. Amalek had hated the people of God for at least the past 400 years and would continue to fight Israel for the next 1,000 years.

As the battle spread out on the plain before Moses, it was not just sword against sword and physical strength against muscle. The battle was spiritual warfare. It was light against darkness, Jehovah against Lucifer.

When Moses lifted his hands in intercession to God, Joshua and Israel prevailed. But because Moses was flesh, he could only keep his arms lifted for a short period of time. When his arms became heavy, he dropped them and Amalek prevailed in battle. But when two intercessors, Aaron and Hur, stood on either side of Moses and held up his hands, God's people defeated the enemy.

The lesson is clear. When intercessors engaged in *warfare-pray*, God's people were victorious. It was only when Moses lacked these prayer partners that the enemy rushed in to overwhelm the forces of God.

What a great lesson! When one man can't intercede alone, God uses two men to help in intercession. Today, if your prayers go unanswered because you prayed solo, learn to *two-pray* with another person. Our theme verse is again at work:

> Again I say to you that if two of you agree on earth concerning anything that they ask, it will be done for them by My Father in heaven (Matt. 18:19).

There are many reasons why we pray, just as there are many methods of praying. Sometimes we *solo-pray* when we have personal requests. At other times we *fellowship-pray* with a partner when we want to enjoy God together. There is time to soak in His presence as we *communion-pray* together. Sometimes we join together to *worship-pray* and magnify the Lord together. At other times, when we are absolutely sure God will answer, we *faith-pray*. Then again there are times when, agonizing as we fight against temptation, addiction or demonic attack, we *warfare-pray* as we wrestle spiritually with the enemy.

WHEN TO *TWO-PRAY*

What are some appropriate times and occasions when *two-pray* is called for?

When You Are Under Attack

Two-pray when you, like Moses, are challenged by the enemy. The victory described above occurred when Israel was crossing the wilderness toward the Promised Land. In the desert, water is more precious than money. God had blessed Israel both spiritually and physically; and Amalek attacked Israel to get the "water rights" of

Horeb that God had given to His people. "Now Amalek came and fought with Israel" (Exod. 17:8).

Have you been attacked lately on either a spiritual or physical front? Launch your counterattack with *two-pray*.

Attacks After Spiritual Blessings

God had just given His people the blessing of water when Amalek attacked. They had begun to grumble because Moses had not supplied them with water. The thirstier they got, the more they complained. Moses cried out to the Lord, asking, "What am I to do with these people?" (Exod. 17:4, *NIV*). In answer to prayer, God gave Moses the solution. He told Moses to take the rod of God and smite the rock at Horeb. Then the Lord said that "water will come out of it for the people to drink" (Exod. 17:6, *NIV*). When Moses obeyed, water instantly gushed out of the rock like a river. The people drank, and rejoiced. Even though they were rejoicing for physical deliverance, still the people understood that it was a spiritual victory. They shouted, "Is the LORD among us, or not?" (Exod. 17:7, *NIV*). It was then, after evidence of God's blessing, that Amalek attacked.

So when you receive a great victory or a great blessing or a great answer to prayer, it is not time to part company with your prayer partner. It is then that you will most likely face a spiritual attack. Are you ready?

Some Battles Are Constant

Because people are creatures of habit, most tend to wrestle with the same problems all their lives. Some people have constant money problems, other people give in to temptations of the flesh, while others are defeated by their pride. Some struggle constantly against drugs, depression or alcohol. At the end of the victory over Amalek, God told Moses, "The LORD will be at war against the Amalekites from generation to generation" (Exod. 17:16, *NIV*). But just as God understood Amalek's violent nature, so He understands our own struggles today.

Therefore, plan to *two-pray* constantly with your friend or prayer partner. Life is a journey. You never quit struggling until you arrive at your destination. You will never quit striving until you arrive at heaven. Forget about a once-and-for-all victory in this life; and forget about perfect tranquillity, where you never have to *warfare-pray* again.

Preparing for Bigger Battles

Your next prayer challenge may be greater than past prayer challenges. Notice that in Israel's case the first problem was to find water in a hot, dusty desert. They faced the threat of dying from thirst. But when Amalek attacked, they faced a second and greater threat of being slaughtered by an old enemy. If given the choice of dying of thirst or by the sword, you would choose to fight rather than surrender to the elements.

Remember that if you have defeated Satan on one day, he will return on a different day, in a different way, to tempt you even more strongly in a different area of your life. Be ready!

PRINCIPLES OF VICTORIOUS INTERCESSION

Victory Comes to the Spiritually Active

God had promised to bless and protect Israel. Yet at the battle at Horeb, God did not give His people the victory just because Joshua and the soldiers geared up for battle. He didn't give them the victory because they were strong or skilled with the sword or for any other physical reason. *God gave them a physical victory because of spiritual intercession.* "When Moses held up his hand . . . Israel prevailed; and when he let down his hand, Amalek prevailed" (Exod. 17:11).

This shows that whatever battle you face, prayer is the single most important thing you can do. Do you have a ministry such as leading a Bible class or any other spiritual responsibility such as your family? Then you can't let up on prayer. What about your job?

Perhaps your company is prospering; don't forget to intercede for personal success on the job, for the future success of your company and for protection from problems or mistakes that would destroy your company. There is a correlation between financial victory and spiritual intercession.

No One Can Win the Battle Alone

Joshua was not able to win the battle alone; He needed Moses' intercession. And Moses was not able to win the spiritual battle alone; he needed Aaron and Hur. "Moses, Aaron, and Hur went up to the top of the hill" (Exod. 17:10).

God uses people according to their talents. Joshua and the soldiers were available to fight the battle with the sword. Moses, the intercessor, used his ministry for spiritual intercession. Both Aaron and Hur were needed to help Moses in intercession. You must recognize your spiritual giftedness and serve according to your ability. Just as there is victory through partnership, so there are answers to prayer when you *two-pray*.

Recognize the Weakness of the Flesh

What stopped Moses' intercession? It was not that he lost interest in praying or that God did not answer. Rather, it was because Moses' hands grew tired and he lowered them (see Exod. 17:10-12). He was not physically able to hold his hands up for a long period of time.

As long as we have human bodies, there will be problems. Some will get sick; they will need friends to *two-pray* for healing. Others are susceptible to temptation; they need friends to intercede for them. Still others serving Christ through the church or on mission fields will face physical limitations; they need friends to *faith-pray* for them.

Just as Moses did, you need physical help when interceding to God. What did the helpers do when the intercession stopped? "They took a stone and put it under him, and he sat on it. And Aaron and Hur supported his hands" (Exod. 17:12). Sometimes your prayers fail because of physical reasons. There are times when you are too cold to keep your mind on prayer. When you get too hot, you faint. If you are an intercessor, you sometimes need a bottle of water nearby to refresh your body, so your spirit can continue in prayer. Sometimes there is a need to fast when praying, and at other times there is a need to eat for strength so you can wrestle in prayer.

And don't forget about those who can't keep their eyes open. Interceders may get sleepy, weak from not eating or exhausted from overwork. In the garden, Jesus told His tired, sleepy disciples, "Watch and pray, lest you enter into temptation. The spirit indeed is willing, but the flesh is weak" (Matt. 26:41).

Leaders need constant help from prayer partners. As Joshua fought Amalek, Moses continued to hold up his arms in intercession with the help of Aaron and Hur. "And his hands were steady until the going down of the sun" (Exod. 17:12). Moses needed help for the entire day.

Don't forget that your pastor needs intercession every day. Those who are fighting spiritual battles need your constant intercession, not once, but continually. For how long? Until the battle is won.

Principles of *Warfare-Prayer*

Victory Is a Team Effort

Who won the victory against Amalek? No *one* did. Joshua defeated the people with the edge of a sword, Moses interceded, and Aaron and Hur held up his arms for him to intercede.

For you to gain a great victory you must learn that "we are God's fellow workers" (1 Cor. 3:9); we are "workers together with Him" (2 Cor. 6:1).

You Need the Proper Tools

Be sure that you make a place for tools in your spiritual warfare. God used humans to fight the battle against Amalek, but humans used instruments to win the war. There were swords in the hands of the soldiers (see Exod. 17:13). They couldn't win the battle without proper tools that were sharp, ready and used with skill.

There was the rod of God in Moses' hand. It stood as a symbol of God's power in Moses' life—it had to be held high. And a stone was needed for Moses to sit on.

In the same way, symbols are important in your own warfare. God uses symbols such as baptism, the Lord's Table and the Cross. Sometimes when you kneel to pray, you need an altar, a rug or a chair on which to lean. Your prayer room at church may need pews for sitting and a rug on the floor for kneeling so that your attention stays focused on prayer.

Your Two Greatest Prayer Challenges

For God to supply your need

For God to supply spiritual protection

The Watchers were a group of intercessors who prayed for Charles Spurgeon at the Metropolitan Baptist Tabernacle in the late 1800s. Because of these intercessors, this became the world-class megachurch of the 1800s. It planted churches throughout England and sent missionaries around the world.

Located in the basement right under the pulpit was a small parlor table with six or seven chairs where these Watchers would kneel. Pillows were kept there to kneel on. Every time Spurgeon preached, the Watchers gathered below him in the basement around the parlor table. It was here that they knelt upon the pillows next to their chairs to intercede so that God would give Spurgeon great power. Over 30 years ago I visited this church and saw the table and chairs that were kept on display in the basement. (I wonder if this church doesn't have its former influence because the chairs are used for display, rather than for prayer.)

Just as Joshua couldn't have won the battle without the inter-cessors on the hill, so Spurgeon would not have had worldwide influence without the Watchers.

Keep a Record of Your Prayer Ministry
After Israel won its great victory over Amalek, God told Moses, "Write this for a memorial" (Exod. 17:14). It is important that you keep records to remind yourself of God's great answers to prayer. Some keep diaries, others keep their actual prayer sheets.

George Mueller built a ministry that became known around the world. During the late 1800s, he cared for over 2,000 orphans in Bristol, England, where he fed, clothed and provided for them by faith. He never asked for an offering. Instead, Mueller was known for his great *faith-pray* ministry. However, twice a year Mueller sent out a booklet to all his prayer partners telling of the great miracles that God had done through the orphanage. These stories and answers to prayers encouraged his prayer partners to pray even more.

In the same way, God reminded Moses to write down the prayer victory over Amalek so that Israel would never forget the role that prayer had played in the establishment of the nation.

Do you have a journal of your prayer victories? Do you have a prayer list where answers are recorded?

Arrange for Memorials
After the battle was over, notice what Moses did to make sure that Israel never forgot that God answered their prayers. "Moses built an altar and called its name, The-LORD-Is-My-Banner [*Jehovah-Nissi*]" (Exod. 17:15). Just as our government places statutes and memori-al stones in public parks to remind us of the past, so Moses con-structed an altar to remind Israel of God's victory.

In the same way, we place plaques and other forms of remem-brances in our churches, so our children will be reminded of past vic-tories. What does this mean to you? Create a journal, written record or some tangible symbol that will memorialize great answers to prayer.

Your Turn Now

Now you've heard about the importance of intercessors. You've seen that even people who pray need help because intercessors wear out and get weary. You've seen the place of tools in spiritual warfare, and of written records and memorials of the victories God gives.

You've seen that one of your most dangerous times is just after you've won a spiritual victory, when the tempter comes after you again with a new attack. So you'll always need intercession and prayer partners. This chapter challenges you to constant vigilance, continual prayer and perfect trust in God. Will you rise to the occasion?

Take-Away Prayer Principles

1. I can win battles when others intercede for me.
2. I should *two-pray* with another when the enemy attacks.
3. I will be attacked right after great spiritual victories.
4. I can win a spiritual battle but not alone.
5. I must recognize the weakness of the flesh in spiritual warfare.
6. I must recognize the place of tools in *warfare-pray*.
7. I should keep a record of answers to prayer for future encouragement.

CHAPTER 4

WHEN YOU
Worship-Pray
EFFECTIVELY

Two-praying was symbolized in the Old Testament by the Tabernacle, the center of worship for God's people when they wandered in the wilderness after the exodus from Egypt.

God told Moses to build a special tent where He would dwell. On one end of this Tabernacle was the Holy of Holies, a small room (10x10 feet), where the Ark of the Covenant was kept. The Ark (which means "box") was something like a precious cedar chest found in many of our own homes. Here are God's instructions for building the Ark:

> You shall make a mercy seat of pure gold for the lid of the ark, it shall be four and a half feet long, and two and a half feet wide. And you shall sculpture two angels of gold; do not mold them. Place one angel at one end of the lid, and the other angel at the other end; they shall be hammered into their final form. And the angels shall stretch out their wings, covering the mercy seat, and they shall face one

another, looking toward God who sits between them on the mercy seat. And I will meet you there, and I will speak with you from the mercy seat, from between the two angels which are on the ark of the Testimony (see Exod. 25:17-20,22.)

WHAT THE ANGELS TEACH ABOUT WORSHIP

We can learn four important principles about worship from the two golden angels atop the Ark:

1. Two angels imply agreement.
2. Pure gold symbolizes holiness.
3. Beaten gold indicates God's handcrafted attention.
4. Spread wings indicate worship.

Remember that as the angels faced each other, they also saw God, who was sitting between them. The lid to the Ark of the Covenant was called the mercy seat, because this is where God would come to sit on the earth, and because it is only by His mercy that He comes at all. He didn't have an earthly throne, so He sat right between the worshiping angels.

What happened when the Tabernacle was finished and the Ark with its mercy seat was set in place? What happened when the two worshiping angels were set in the Holy of Holies? What happened when God's people sanctified themselves and worshiped God? *He came to receive their worship.* Then God's glory cloud covered the Tabernacle, and God's presence filled the Tabernacle. Moses and the priest were not able to enter because the glory of God filled the place (see Exod. 40:34-35).

It was as though God told all heaven to be silent so that he could come to earth and listen to those who were worshiping Him. Instantly, the glory-cloud of God's presence left heaven to sweep down to Earth in a smoking cloud of fire. "Look out! Here He comes!" was the message Moses gave to the people.

Do you want God in your life? He will come to receive your praise at the place where you worship Him. Jesus told us that the Father seeks worship from worshipers (see John 4:23). If you haven't experienced the presence of God, you should ask whether you have prepared a place for God to visit your life.

The same thing happened after worship in the Tabernacle gave way to worship at the Temple Solomon built. At the Temple's dedication the message again was "Watch God come!" "When Solomon had finished praying, fire came down from heaven and consumed the burnt offering . . . and the glory of the LORD filled the temple" (2 Chron. 7:1). Swoosh! God instantly appeared to receive the praise offered by His servant.

I have had the same thing happen in a drab motel room. (All motel rooms look the same, and none of them is as nice as sleeping in my own bedroom.) There have been times when I've come in late and didn't get enough sleep. The next morning my bones would ache, and even a cup of coffee and my regular routine of praying the Lord's Prayer and reading the Bible couldn't awaken my spirit. Perhaps it was a cold, cloudy day, when even the walls seemed wet with humidity.

But when I bowed my head to the Lord in worship, praising Him for His greatness and goodness, my drab sleeping room would be transformed into a sanctuary. Any room is a sanctuary if God is there. And when His presence entered the motel room, it would change my outlook for that day. After such experiences, how could I begin any day without worshiping the Lord?

Two Angels Imply Agreement

Why were there two angels on the Ark of the Covenant? I think they remind us of *two-pray* and *two-worship*. The Ark of the Covenant was the place where God visited His people and the two symbolic angels were as close as possible to the presence of God. This reminds us that two worshipers should agree to continually sing, with the angels of heaven, "Holy, holy, holy is the LORD of hosts; the whole earth is full of His glory!" (Isa. 6:3). Even before Jesus told us to agree with another in prayer—i.e., *two-pray*—God the Father arranged for two symbolic prayer-worshipers to be placed over the mercy seat on the Ark of the Covenant. These two angels tell us that it is important to *worship-pray* with another person.

So, with whom do you praise God?

Why *two* angels, instead of one or three? There could have been one angel representing God's unity. There could have been three angels to symbolize the Trinity, the Father, Son and the Holy Spirit.

Two is the Bible number of witnesses for credibility. "By the mouth of two . . . witnesses the matter shall be established" (Deut. 19:15). Two witnesses verify that a statement is true. The two angels on the Ark testify to the truth that God is worthy of praise and worship.

Would you be more effective in prayer if you had a partner to verify your witness?

Just as the two angels look at each other and at God, so you agree with your prayer partner as you look to God. Isn't this a good example for prayer? If one prayer partner tries to worship or pray with the wrong words, wrong attitude or wrong purpose, the other would not verify what was said. It takes two intercessors to pray honestly, with honest prayer motives, with honest prayer requests and with an honest desire for the glory of God.

If you are not experiencing God's presence in your life, maybe you aren't trying to get His attention in the right way. You go to church in your humdrum way, waiting for God to break through your time warp, to come beat down the door of your life like police beating down a door in a drug bust. God could crash into your life like that, but that's not His usual *modus operandi*. He usually waits to be wanted. The Lord tells us, "Seek Me while I can be found" (see Jer. 29:13).

So how does the Lord get you to search for Him? He permits persecution, fire or loss, so you will cry out for Him. "You will seek Me and find Me, when you search for Me with all your heart" (Jer. 29:13). When you seek God in worship, you will find Him on His mercy seat, between the worshiping angels.

Pure Gold Suggests Holiness

The two angels weren't just made of gold but of *pure* gold. Gold has several degrees of purity. There are rings of 10-karat and 24-karat gold; and everyone knows that the most expensive gold is the purest. God told Moses to make the angels of pure gold, because God wants purity in the lives of those who worship Him.

The difference between pure gold and a lesser grade of gold is *fire*. And the hotter the purifying fire, the more dross and impurities are burned away. As the fire is heated, the gold melts and the sludge floats to the top where it is skimmed away, leaving refined gold.

Because God wants those closest to Him to be holy, He adds the fire of suffering and difficulties of life to the intercessors to rid them of their impurities. And those who are closest to Him get the most attention. Sometimes He allows financial reverses to strike devoted believers so they will go immediately to Him in prayer. Because of imminent financial disaster, they cry out honestly to God in prayer. And while they are crying to God and seeking His presence, they are releasing their covetous grip on material welfare. Fire burns away the impurity of their greed.

Do you have any impurities that need to be burned away? Do you feel fire licking around the edges of an unyielding possession? Don't complain to God, nor doubt Him. Don't think that He doesn't love you. Instead, let your prayer be, "O God, do Your work in my life!" Let His purifying fire upgrade you into pure gold.

When gold is first put into the goldsmith's fire, the heat burns away the dirtiest impurities, including trash and filth. The same process happens in the Christian life. God first touches our fleshly sins, our sexual sins and our outward problems.

Next, the goldsmith turns up the flame, so the fire can burn away unseen impurities. Again, the same thing happens in the life of the believer. After you've been separated from outward sins, God then focuses on inward sins that hinder your walk with Him. The fire of conviction burns away unseen impurities of attitude and desires, little things you allow to block your communion with God.

Often, the goldsmith working with ore finds that the last element to be burned away is silver! "But, silver is good," you say. Yes, silver is considered a precious metal; but even silver must be burned away if you want pure gold.

Let silver stand for the good things you do for God and others—your good works. But what is it that you do for God that is more important than God Himself? Do you let such "silver" get in the way of knowing God Himself? If it does, your silver must be burned away before you become pure gold.

So why did God demand that the angels and the mercy seat be made of pure gold? Because God Himself is sitting with them right there on the mercy seat. Since He is a pure God, He would not sit there if the mercy seat and the angels were made of impure gold.

How pure is pure gold, and how does the goldsmith know the gold is pure? You can't tell how pure the gold is just by looking at it. Pureness is not determined by how long you leave gold in the fire or how big the flames are. Only when all dross is gone is the gold pure; and the goldsmith will know when the gold is at that pure stage only by looking into the golden liquid as he would look into a mirror, to see his face. When he sees himself in the gold, then he knows the gold is pure.

Likewise, when God looks into your soul and sees Himself, then He knows you are pure gold. Why does God allow the flames of trials in your life? He's burning away dross, so He can see Himself in your life.

Today, who does God see when He looks into your heart? You—or Himself?

Beaten Gold Indicates God's Handcrafted Attention

The two worshiping angels were sculpted from one piece of gold—not poured into a mold but beaten into form. The were shaped and crafted by hand into the proper form. And the purer the gold, the easier it was to sculpt as the craftsman intended.

This reminds us that worshipers are not formed easily or cheaply. They are literally shaped by God's hands into the worshiping position. To be beaten is not the same thing as to be purified. When you are pure, it means you have separated yourself from sin, i.e., you are holy. Being sculpted means you have yielded to God's will and have put your life in His hands.

We are also reminded that all things that are poured into the same mold become indentical. The toy soldiers I played with as a boy were all identical because they came out of the same mold. But when you sculpt something, it is unique. A sculptor cannot beat two images into identical shape. Each is a little different from the other. So, as God forms us into worshipers, each of us is a little different from the other, although all of us are fashioned by the hands of the same Master Craftsman.

And don't forget that while cheap imitations can be made by pouring liquid into a mold, a genuine work of art is sculptured by a master craftsman. He puts his personality and talent into what he forms. So God, the Master Craftsman, puts unique life, *His* life and design, into us, when He molds us into worshipers.

Can you see the goldsmith shaping a worshiping angel? Is a wing not lifted correctly in praise? A few touches from the Master's hand will bring it into the proper place. Perhaps the head is not bowed as it should be. A touch of the right tool, the right hammer, will correct the problem.

What kind of hammer does God use on you? He always has the right kind of tool to use on the unique problem of pride. He might use a different hammer on greed and an entirely different hammer on lust. Because my problems are different from yours, God will use a different hammer on me than on you. He has all kinds of hammers for all kinds of problems. He uses His tools on our gold until each of us is just right—just right for worship.

If you won't allow the Lord to use His hammer on you, then something else or someone else will have to beat you into submission. If you are beaten by the world, the flesh and the Devil, you can end up broken—in body and spirit, perhaps for your whole life. That's not God's plan. He doesn't beat you to crush you. No! God uses His hammer to mold you into a true worshiper. He doesn't want to break you but to bend your heart to His will, to enable you to look more like Him. "But we all, with unveiled face, beholding as in a mirror the glory of the Lord, are being transformed into the same image from glory to glory, just as by the Spirit of the Lord" (2 Cor. 3:18).

How willing are you to be shaped by God into His image?

Spread Wings Mean Worship

God told Moses that if he would build the Tabernacle according to the blueprint of heaven, He would dwell there (see Exod. 25:8-9). God promises He will come down to sit on the mercy seat between the two angels. Why there? Because God loves worship, He comes to sit between the worship of two angels, two beings who agree to *worship-pray.*

The two worshiping angels of pure gold are symbolic of a vast number of other heavenly beings who surround God constantly saying, "Holy, holy, holy" (Isa. 6:3). Remember that God loves symbols because they stand for a heavenly reality. Like the cross that reflects His substitutionary sacrifice of love for your sins, the two worshiping angels on the Ark are just symbols to remind us to worship God, so we will find His presence.

The angels with outstretched wings remind us of worshipers stretching out their hands in praise to God. God consented to dwell at the mercy seat in the Tabernacle not just because Moses followed the blueprint to the letter of the Law, and not because of the expensive gold appointments. He dwelt there because, as the angel's outspread wings symbolized, praise to Him was being offered; and the Lord came down to live in the praises of Israel (see Ps. 22:3).

When was the last time you spread your hands in worship to God?

So the angels on the Ark of the Covenant in the Tabernacle, and then the Temple, remind us of the importance of worship and of *two-pray.* Before you ask for something, make sure you worship the Lord first, so He will visit your prayer with His presence, meeting you to hear your requests. He'll come if you praise Him.

YOUR TURN NOW

You can transform any listless quiet time by worshiping God, because He will come to you if you worship Him. If you will worship together with your prayer partner, God will enthrone Himself in your praise.

When you have trouble getting answers to prayer, even when you have met all the conditions for prayer, perhaps you are beginning to ask before God comes to listen. You need to learn to worship God first, so His presence will be felt as you pray. Remember to *worship-pray* before you *two-pray* or even *intercede-pray*.

Worship, however, isn't a gimmick. Never use worship as a technique to get your prayers answered. God will not be manipulated. He comes to us in worship because He longs for a relationship with us. We lift outstretched arms to Him because we love Him, and in order to honor Him as the One who means more to us than anything else in our lives.

Remember the lesson of spread wings.

TAKE-AWAY PRAYER PRINCIPLES

1. I can transform my quiet time with worship.
2. I am reminded to worship with another person by the symbol of the two angels on the Ark.
3. I will let pressures and fiery trials purify me.
4. I will let God's hammer shape me into a worshiper.
5. I should lift my hands and spread my arms in worship to God.
6. I may not have my prayers answered because I am not worshiping before asking.

CHAPTER 5

WHEN YOU
Faith-Pray
TOGETHER FOR MINISTRY

I was scared the first time I was asked to preach, because it wasn't in a safe church sanctuary to a group of Christians on a Sunday morning. It was at a street meeting on the corners of Main and Ervey Streets in downtown Columbia, South Carolina, on a Saturday night in February 1951. I was 18 years old, eager to preach; but I was fearful, stumbling, rambling—and at times incoherent.

FAITH-PRAYING: FAILURE AND SUCCESS

Before I preached, I had attended the street meetings every Saturday night for five months, along with 9 or 10 other young students from Columbia Bible College. We would begin the evening by spreading out over the streets of downtown Columbia, each one of us meeting soldiers from Camp Jackson, a nearby military base, to invite them to come to the meeting.

The soldiers were just walking the streets in small groups, trying to avoid boredom on a Saturday evening. Each one of us would make friends with a group of soldiers and invite them to the street meeting where they would hear the gospel and, we hoped, become converted to Christ.

I knew that each one of the students from the Bible college would have a chance to preach, but they kept putting me off because I was the youngest and least experienced. Finally, in February, when they couldn't come up with any more excuses, I got my chance.

Because I wanted God to do something special in my first sermon, I asked Gladdie Kreimann, the student song leader of the evening, to fast and pray with me at lunchtime every day for five days before the meeting at which I was to preach. We met in the school prayer room to beg God for His power to convert soldiers at the street meeting. I didn't understand the power of *two-pray* then, nor did I understand the power of fasting; all I wanted was God's power on the meeting.

When Saturday night finally arrived, it was a bitter-cold evening with howling winds sweeping through the canyonlike streets between the buildings of downtown Columbia. Only three students showed up for the meeting—Gladdie and a young man who played the pump organ and I. We fanned out to invite soldiers to come to the meeting, but because of the cold very few soldiers were walking the streets. We only got four soldiers to attend.

It was so cold that Gladdie only led two or three hymns—very weakly. Then he led in prayer and turned the meeting over to me. His part had taken less than five minutes, and he expected me to take additional time with the sermon. I stood in front of the seven shivering forms, and with my squeaky, immature voice, I shouted the Scripture verse as loud as I could, to compete with the wind.

I launched into my sermon, expecting to preach for 20 or 30 minutes. I don't remember how many points I had, but they weren't enough. I repeated my points two or three times—and it took me a whole four minutes to preach my sermon. (Later I would remember the words of Abraham Lincoln: "Be careful of speaking up to the edge of your knowledge. You might fall off." That night I fell off the edge of an ill-prepared sermon because I hadn't studied deeply or widely.)

I started into the invitation. I think the soldiers knew that I was a novice when I invited them to walk five or six feet to take my hand and be saved. No one moved. We sang two verses and still nothing happened, except my face grew redder and redder—not from the cutting wind but from the embarrassment of failure. No one had to tell me that it was a terrible sermon. But as I raised my hand to give the benediction I was interrupted by a bombastic voice: "May I give a word of testimony?"

I hadn't seen this large man, almost seven feet tall, step out of the shadows from the back where the soldiers were standing. Pushing his way through the "boys," he took my place and with a loud dramatic voice began to quote whole chapters from the book of Isaiah. He quoted passages about the coming kingdom of God, about the approaching Day of Judgment, about personal repentance and about salvation.

Soon a small crowd had gathered, captivated by the big man's voice. Groups of soldiers drifted over to the street meeting, partly to get out of the bitter wind, I'm sure. The man's bronze complexion, high cheekbones and black hair combed straight back told me he was a Native American. His gigantic hand gestured, almost seeming to reach across the distance between preacher and audience and draw people to himself as he said, "You need to be saved . . . now!"

The crowd had grown to between 30 and 50 people. As I remember, cars pulled over to the curb and people hung out their rolled-down windows to listen—a couple of cars even double-parked in the street, so the occupants could hear. After preaching for more than 30 minutes, the passionate Native American gave a command, instead of an invitation. He pointed to the sidewalk and demanded, "Come and kneel; come and repent; come and call on the Lord Jesus Christ!"

Soldiers actually leaped forward and fell to their knees on the stony, cold pavement. Just as quickly, these three boys from Columbia

Bible College began leading repentant soldiers to pray the Sinner's Prayer. I left one kneeling soldier to turn to another, and another and another . . . As I remember, 18 people prayed to receive Christ that night. When the last soldier was converted, I looked around for the Native American evangelist; but he was gone. He had stepped out of the black night, preached one of the most powerful sermons I've ever heard in my life and disappeared just as quickly.

I learned three important lessons that evening that have stuck with me. First, it's amazing what God can do if we don't care who gets the credit. Second, when two young boys agreed in prayer that soldiers would get saved, God in heaven heard their prayer and answered. Third, when God has a big task to do, He may choose to use a gifted, Spirit-filled man of God with experience instead of a young, inexperienced preacher.

PETER AND JOHN *FAITH-PRAY* FOR MINISTRY

The third chapter of Acts records an incident illustrating the power of faith-praying for ministry. It begins by saying simply: "Now Peter and John went up together to the temple at the hour of prayer, the ninth hour" (Acts 3:1). Peter and John were used mightily of God because they were in the habit of praying. Here God used them to heal a beggar, crippled from birth, who had been at the entrance of the Temple for more than 40 years. Because of this miracle, Peter and John were summoned before the Sanhedrin, where they testified to the exclusive offer of salvation in Jesus Christ. What can we learn from this relatively unknown habit of praying together, that led to such great opportunities for ministry?

They Planned to Pray Together
Obviously, Peter and John could have prayed individually, and much is said throughout Scripture about seeking God alone in "the prayer closet."

As powerful as it is to pray alone, however, these apostles felt it was important for them to pray *together*. As convenient as it is to pray alone, these disciples went to the trouble to plan to go together to the Temple. Who can deny that a marvelous outcome resulted from this conscious choice?

Have you *planned* to pray regularly with another person? Who can tell whether a similar glorious ministry might result?

They Planned to Pray at a Specific Place

Obviously, Peter and John could have prayed elsewhere in the city. Hadn't they recently prayed in the Upper Room with the other disciples? As a matter of fact, they had prayed there for 10 days between the Ascension and Pentecost. They had also prayed as they went from house to house breaking bread (see Acts 2:46). Yet at this time they chose to pray together at the Temple.

There is an advantage in setting a specific place for prayer. In the Old Testament it was the custom for the people to pray at the Temple daily. People were not required to attend this meeting; but after the event of the Cross and Resurrection, perhaps Peter and John were going to offer prayers for the lost people of the world and ask that God would help them carry out the Great Commission. Whatever their reason, they thought it important to come to a specific place to pray.

Do you have a regular place for prayer?

They Prayed at a Particular Time

It was the Jewish custom to offer prayer at the Temple at 3 P.M. daily. It was then that the appointed priest went into the Holy Place to offer prayers for all Israel. Having a particular time to pray ensures that praying occurs. People who plan to pray when they "get around to it" seldom pray. Those who have a specific time to pray are more likely to spend more time in prayer. Peter and John are your example to make and keep an appointment to *two-pray*.

When will you pray?

They Had Formed a Habit of Praying Together

When the Bible says Peter and John "went up together" (Acts 3:1), the original language suggests that they were in the habit of continuously going up together. Praying together was something they did routinely. But it was more than a habit. Outwardly, prayer was a discipline; inwardly, it was a passion every day.

How can you get God to answer your prayer—to give you power—before you ask for it? By making a commitment to God to meet Him at a certain time each day. Sometimes when you don't know how to pray for the right thing, God sees the commitment of your heart to meet Him each day, and He will meet with you and answer you, even when you don't know what to ask. And when you continually pray at the appointed time in an appointed place, you form a habit of prayer.

How disciplined is your prayer ministry?

They Were Obeying the Right Priority

Often you are faced with the question of how to spend your time serving the Lord. Some honestly feel that they need to spend more time serving Christ than praying to Him. Because your ministry needs are so urgent, time spent meeting those needs may eclipse your prayer time, resulting in the neglect of prayer. Notice in this text that Peter and John made prayer a priority. Their circumstances made their decision to pray more amazing. On the recent Day of Pentecost, 3,000 were added to the Church. They had momentum. We know this because:

> People were praying everywhere (see Acts 2:42).
> New converts were studying the apostles' doctrine (see
>   Acts 2:42).
> Apostles were doing many signs and wonders (see Acts
>   2:43).
> The believers shared all things in common (see Acts 2:44).
> The church had the favor of the city (see Acts 2:47).

In spite of all this momentum and growth, Peter and John retreated to the Temple to pray. Some might have questioned why they left the excitement of evangelism to go to a secluded place to pray. Others might have thought they were compromising, because they were leaving ministry to the other disciples. Some may have thought that by attending Temple prayers Peter and John were fellowshiping with the enemy and showing too much reverence for Old Testament ways that had been put aside by the death of Christ. Still others may have thought they were not spending enough time with the infant Church. But no matter what others may have thought, Peter and John made prayer a priority.

DON'T WORRY ABOUT PRAYERS THAT ARE NOT ANSWERED

WORRY ABOUT THE PRAYERS THAT ARE NOT OFFERED

The massive journals of John Wesley (close to 22 volumes) show how busy he was every day doing the work of God. He went by horseback from city to city, preaching constantly and nurturing the new churches he was founding. But in the face of all these pressures, Wesley acknowledged, "I have so much to do that I can't get it done if I don't spend two hours in prayer every day."[1]

My good friend David Yonggi Cho pastors the largest church in the world—the largest in history—and we can all imagine how busy his schedule is. He has over 760,000 members in the Yoido Full Gospel Church in Seoul, South Korea. Each week more than 70,000 small groups, called cells, meet in homes, recreational buildings, apartment buildings and restaurants throughout the city. He oversees a vast empire of hospitals, schools, orphanages and a citywide newspaper, plus all the daily care of the believers. Yet, he begins each day with *two hours* of prayer.

Recently I phoned to invite Pastor Cho for breakfast, because I was teaching a seminary class in Seoul from 8 A.M. to 5 P.M. He delayed his morning prayer time to meet me for breakfast. But he told me, "I will spend two hours praying this afternoon, not because I have to but because I want to, and because I missed it this morning. Prayer is the greatest way I serve my church." I apologized for drawing him away, thinking he would get so many interruptions during the day that he wouldn't get around to his prayer time. But he said, "I interrupt my time with people to spend time with God; most people interrupt their time with God to spend time with people."

They Were Given a New Opportunity for Service

Because Peter and John put prayer in its appropriate place, God gave them a new opportunity in Christian service:

> And a certain man lame from his mother's womb was carried, whom they laid daily at the gate of the temple which is called Beautiful, to ask alms from those who entered the temple; who, seeing Peter and John about to go into the temple, asked for alms (Acts 3:2).

Can you see the man sitting beside the gate? As you approached Jerusalem from the east and the Kidron Valley, you entered the city through the Golden Gate (also called the Eastern Gate). Once inside, you saw the beautiful Temple stretching out before you. Across a large courtyard was the Beautiful Gate, which is the main entrance into the Temple.

Because no one with a physical deformity could enter the Temple, this crippled man had never been inside to hear the Levitical choirs, bring his sacrifice to God or eat his peace offering with the Levites in the courtyard of the Temple. So he sat on the steps and begged alms from those entering the Temple. (He wisely perceived that most people who come to worship are also willing to open their pocketbooks.) But neither the crippled man nor his benefactors realized what a marvelous gift he was about to receive. Today, through the ministry of Peter and John, this man's life would be changed forever.

Do you pray with the expectation that God will give you a new opportunity for ministry?

They Were Given New Power for Service

The crippled man was the first to make contact. "Seeing Peter and John about to go into the Temple, [he] asked for alms" (Acts 3:3). How could Peter and John say no to this request? When you open up your heart in prayer to God, you also open up your heart to others. Perhaps Peter fumbled through the bag he carried, looking for a coin before realizing that he was broke. But because prayer gives us confidence to serve God, Peter determined to do something anyway. "And fixing his eyes on him, with John, Peter said, 'Look at us'" (v. 4).

In saying this, Peter appealed to the crippled man's curiosity. The man must already have been looking at the apostles, but Peter wanted him to look with the expectation of receiving something greater than money. We don't know how close it was to the 3 P.M. prayers when Peter met the lame man, but he and John were going to be a few minutes late. God was going to do a miracle through Peter, because God uses people who will interrupt their schedule for Him.

The crippled man would have been sitting in the shadows, because the Beautiful Gate faces east, and at 3 P.M. the sun would have been sinking towards the western horizon on the other side of Herod's Temple. Symbolically, maybe the man felt that his life was slipping into the shadows, too. Maybe this was his last opportunity to encounter God and receive healing.

When Peter commanded, "Look at us," the crippled man looked up expecting a handout (see v. 5). He didn't realize that he would get God's hand *up* to walk again. But Peter spoke with confidence: "Silver and gold I do not have, but what I do have I give you: In the name of Jesus Christ of Nazareth, rise up and walk" (v. 6).

Too often we let *immediate* needs overshadow *ultimate* needs. We let our need for money, things or possessions crowd out the most important need of all: to touch God and be touched by Him. Peter looked beyond the man's request for money to deal with his crippled feet and his ultimate need for Christ in his life.

God uses those who are inspired to help others. What did Peter and John have? A life of disciplined prayer. Because they were men of prayer, they would give the man that which filled their life: Jesus Christ of Nazareth.

God also uses those who know what they *cannot* do. Peter and John knew they could not help the man financially. They also knew that it was not in their power to heal the man—the power was "in the name of Jesus Christ of Nazareth." The first step in Christian service is to realize that you can't minister in your own strength. You must come to the end of yourself before you can rely wholly on God to work a miracle. Because Peter had immersed himself in prayer, he had anticipatory faith and could say with confidence, "Rise up and walk."

Note, however, that nothing appeared to happen at first. So Peter took the man by the hand and pulled him up off the ground (see v. 7). An observer may have tried to stop Peter, saying, "Obviously the healing words haven't worked. Don't embarrass yourself and the crippled man. Leave him alone." But Peter had already made a faith statement; and he responded to it in faith by reaching out and helping the man to his feet. "And immediately his feet and ankle bones received strength" (v. 7). The miracle didn't take place until Peter's work joined with his words.

What a beautiful picture of partnership with God! Are you anticipating that through your *faith-praying* and faith-saying God will give you new power?

They Had Learned a New Discipline

Think of how this amazing miracle must have affected the future prayer life of Peter and John. They had applied to a specific situation a principle Jesus had taught earlier, "If two of you agree on earth concerning anything that they ask, it will be done for them by My Father in heaven" (Matt. 18:19). However, it remained for the two disciples to put this principle into practice. They did so in the ways we have mentioned—*two-praying, faith-praying* for ministry, having the discipline to pray at a specific time and place, and expecting new opportunity and power for ministry.

The discipline of praying together invited God into a situation on the Temple steps—an invitation that can become a pattern for us today.

Learning Prayer-Discipline from Peter and John
Discipline enables us to pray together.
Discipline brings us to pray at a particular place.
Discipline helps us to pray at a specific time.
Discipline causes us to pray for a specific purpose.
Discipline inspires us to give priority to prayer.
Discipline is rewarded by opportunity for ministry.
Discipline results in power in ministry.
Discipline teaches us the power of discipline!

Do you have this kind of discipline?

YOUR TURN NOW

Now you can enter a new realm of ministry. How do you serve the Lord? Are you a preacher, teacher, counselor or speaker? Are you a Christian parent striving to raise your children right? Then determine to find a prayer partner and discipline yourself to pray with them at a scheduled place and a scheduled time. Learn the joy of *two-pray* and *faith-pray*, so you can receive God's blessing on your ministry.

What is the greatest thief of your time? Is it lack of a schedule, too many jobs or no job description? Perhaps it is a lack of discipline or an inadequate focus on priorities. Whatever your time problem, it probably shows up most dramatically in loss of prayer time. What can you do?

Revise your priorities and schedule. Place prayer first and then fit other things into your "to do" list. Out of the discipline of prayer, you will discover the most important priority in life. Then, let prayer govern your schedule for the rest of the day.

TAKE-AWAY PRAYER PRINCIPLES

1. I can establish a prayer relationship with someone to *two-pray* for my ministry.
2. I can set a regular time and place for *two-pray*.
3. I will receive great opportunities for ministry when I effectively *two-pray*.
4. I will get spiritual power in ministry if I *two-pray* with another.
5. I can turn mundane experiences into ministry opportunities if I am spiritually ready for them.
6. After I have spoken the Word of God, as in "Rise and walk," I have to act on my faith by "taking the man by the hand."

WHEN YOU
Fellowship-Pray
IN DIFFICULTIES

My wife and I were transfer students to Northwestern College in Minneapolis. If we had not prayed together daily through all our difficulties, I don't know how we would have made it.

The first pressure was living in the northern social climate, because I was from the South. Second, we didn't have the heavier clothing needed to survive the cold winters. Third, I earned $1 an hour for driving a school bus, which was just enough to pay for our necessities; but there wasn't even a dime left over for a Coca-Cola.

One evening, the only thing in the kitchen cabinet was a can of tuna fish, so my wife served a tuna casserole. As we clasped hands to thank God for the food, I prayed, "God, You know we are broke. You know it's two days until payday. You know we are willing to fast until we get money, but we ask You to please take care of our needs."

As we finished praying, the laundry man came to the door. Ruth met him to say, "No laundry today, we can't afford to have anything cleaned." But he had not come to pick up our cleaning. The laundry man explained, "A few months ago your landlord asked me to pass along $20 to you to pay for your having thawed the pipes for him. I had forgotten about it until today." Some might say this was a coincidence, but Ruth and I say that our prayer together—*two-pray*—reminded the laundry man that he had $20 for us. He had been sent by God.

TWO-PRAYING IN PRISON

Paul and Silas had come to Philippi to preach the gospel and begin a church. A young girl in the city had a demon that apparently enabled her to tell fortunes. She recognized that Paul and Silas were sent by God, so she trailed after them yelling, "These men are the servants of the Most High God, who proclaim to us the way of salvation" (Acts 16:17).

After several days, Paul cast the demon out of the girl. When the girl's owners realized that they had lost their source of income, they had Paul and Silas thrown in jail. Then, in the middle of the night as Paul and Silas prayed—*two-praying*—God answered in a miraculous way. There are eight principles that can be applied to *two-pray* when you face difficulties.

1. *Two-Pray* Despite Conditions

Paul and Silas were not just cast into prison, they were thrown into the worst place in prison, the inner prison, and their feet were fastened in the stocks (see Acts 16:24).

If your days are dark and you face a reversal, this is the best time for *two-pray* to begin. When you think that prayer won't work, or that it's too late to pray or that God can't do anything, remind yourself that "with God nothing will be impossible" (Luke 1:37). Like Paul and Silas, *two-pray* when your conditions are the worst.

2. *Two-Pray* to See God's Presence

What was Paul's and Silas's response to persecution? The Bible uses the verb *proseuchomai*, which indicates that they were continuously praying. They were turning to the face of God in their times of difficulty.

Technically, this word for prayer suggests they were not asking God to do anything for them. Synonyms for this word mean "talking" and "having fellowship" with God, having "communion" with Him and "abiding" in Him. There are times when you come to the Lord not to ask Him for anything, but just to talk to Him and enjoy His presence.

My pastor, Jerry Falwell, who is also chancellor of Liberty University, once prayed and fasted for 40 days for money. God kept telling him, "Don't try to get into My pocketbook, find My heart." My pastor had to learn the importance of just being in God's presence before He could intercede for the financial needs of the university.

If you have problems, *two-pray* to Him about them now—and expect just to enjoy His presence.

3. *Two-Pray* Instead of Sleeping
Think about the situation. Paul and Silas had been beaten, and now they were in the innermost prison with their feet locked in the stocks. There was nothing they could do. Their backs were bleeding, and they couldn't even lie down. Have you ever ached so badly that you couldn't sleep? Paul and Silas couldn't, so they prayed.

The next time you are worried about your problems and can't sleep, get up and pray. God gives you sleep when you are weary. Each night I pray, and then "I lie down and sleep" (Ps. 3:5, *NIV*). But God may also awaken you for a purpose. When He does that, you should arise to pray for things that frighten or worry you.

4. *Two-Pray* Instead of Complaining
Paul and Silas had every right to complain. They had broken no law, yet they were locked up. They had told the truth, yet they had been flogged. They knew they were innocent, and on the following morning they would put fear into the authorities for their having been treated unjustly as Roman citizens. They *lived* what the apostle Paul

would later write to his friends in this very city: "Be anxious for nothing, but in everything by prayer and supplication, with thanksgiving, let your requests be made known to God" (Phil. 4:6).

WHAT PAUL AND SILAS DIDN'T PRAY

They didn't complain to God in prayer.
They didn't call down wrath on the authorities.
They didn't try to cast out the demons around them.
They didn't ask for the authorities to change their minds.
They didn't ask God to get them out of jail.

Those in Philippi who became Christians could believe what Paul wrote because he modeled it in their hometown one dark night. Paul and Silas *two-prayed* together instead of complaining.

5. *Two-Pray* in Worship

In the middle of the night as Paul and Silas were praying they were also "singing hymns to God" (Acts 16:25). The word for "singing" here is from *humneo*, from which we derive our word for "hymn." Paul and Silas were "hymning" there in the jail at night.

The Early Church used at least three types of music, "psalms and hymns and spiritual songs" (Col. 3:16). Hymns were sung in adoration and praise of God (see the *King James Version*, which says Paul and Silas "sang praises unto God" [Acts 16:25]). They were not singing a song of complaint to God. Instead, they were praising God even though they were in dire circumstances.

In the darkness of the dungeon, Paul and Silas were magnifying God instead of focusing on their circumstances. Humanly speaking, their condition was so terrible that they could not be expected to praise God, but they did it anyway. Not only did the other prisoners hear them; those hymns also drifted out of the jail all the way into the throne room of God. And as we shall see, God jumped up from His throne and rushed down to the jail where His disciples were *two-praying*!

Think about the last time you were in trouble. Did you *two-pray* in praise to God?

6. When You *Two-Pray,* You Obey Scripture

Let's look more closely at what Paul and Silas must have been singing. In Matthew 26:30, Jesus and His disciples sang a hymn after they celebrated the Passover. The Jewish custom was to select this hymn from the Hallel, the praise Psalms 113—118. So when Paul and Silas sang a hymn, they may well have selected just such a psalm of praise. Perhaps they were singing, "This is the day the LORD has made; we will rejoice and be glad in it" (Ps. 118:24).

Since God makes every day and places us in a specific day for a specific purpose, what else can we do but rejoice in that day? That was Paul's and Silas's response on the day they were thrown into prison.

7. *Two-Pray* Results in Deliverance

"Suddenly there was a great earthquake . . . immediately all the doors were opened and everyone's chains were loosed" (Acts 16:26). It was as though God said to the angels, "Listen to my servants praising Me!" and then rushed to their rescue. Many think that the earthquake shook the doors open so Paul and Silas could get out. Perhaps not! Maybe the doors were opened so that God could get in to enjoy the worship! Of course that's a figure of speech, because God is present everywhere, and He can go through stone walls and locked prison doors. But the metaphor is used to show that God inhabits the praises of His people Israel (see Ps. 22:3).

Not only were Paul and Silas praying, but the members of the young church at Philippi were also praying. Probably they were in Lydia's home, because as a businesswoman who sold purple fabric, she probably had the largest house, one that could hold all the church members. When Paul and Silas were released, they went to Lydia's house where the church had gathered, and "when they had seen the brethren, they encouraged them" (Acts 16:40). Because the church had worried, prayed and expressed their fears in intercession, Paul and Silas showed up to demonstrate to them how God had answered their prayers.

Are you satisfied with the results of your prayers?

8. *Two-Praying* Leads Others to Christ

Because Paul and Silas prayed that night, the Philippian jailer and his household were converted. The jailer would have lived in a room in the prison, or on the second floor above the prison or in a house next door. Throughout the night when he made his rounds to check up on his prisoners, he would have heard their singing. Perhaps the prayers of Paul and Silas drifted into his house; and in any case the earthquake jarred him to the realization that something unusual had happened.

IS IT TRUE THAT WHEN YOU WORSHIP GOD HE WILL BREAK DOWN THE DOORS TO GET INSIDE TO HEAR YOUR PRAISE?

When the jailer came into the prison and saw that the doors were opened and the shackles on all the prisoners were loosed, he drew out his sword to kill himself. As the keeper of the prison, he was responsible for the prisoners, and if any were to escape, his life would be forfeited. He thought that it would be better to die by his own hands than face the rebuke and humiliation of his superiors.

But Paul cried out through the night, "Do yourself no harm, for we are all here" (Acts 16:28). Carrying a light, the jailer ran throughout the prison to count heads. When he realized that none was missing, he brought Paul and Silas out and fell down before them asking, "What must I do to be saved?" (v. 30).

Paul and Silas answered, "Believe on the Lord Jesus Christ, and you will be saved, you and your household" (v. 31).

This simple statement has become one of the universal declarations of the gospel. How easy is it for a person to be converted? All one has to do is believe on the Lord Jesus Christ and he or she shall be saved!

Several things happened next. First, the jailer took them to his house, washed their stripes and gave them something to eat. As his wounds were being washed, Paul preached the gospel to the jailer and all his family. That night the jailer and his family were baptized as a testimony of their personal belief in Jesus Christ. Then they all rejoiced together because they believed in the Lord Jesus Christ (see vv. 33-34).

The next morning the authorities came down to release Paul and Silas and send them on their way. But Paul had a challenge for them: "They have beaten us openly, uncondemned Romans, and have thrown us into prison. And now do they put us out secretly? No indeed! Let them come themselves and get us out" (v. 37).

Paul uses his citizenship advantage for the establishment of the new Church. The authorities came down and gave Paul and Silas their freedom. A permissive attitude by the authorities allowed the young Philippian church to grow and prosper. Later when Paul writes to the church, he finds nothing to condemn; and the Philippians continue to minister to him throughout his life (see Phil. 1:3-5).

YOUR TURN NOW

You get to apply these lessons when you face a problem or go through a dangerous situation. First, when troubles come, turn to your prayer partner to *two-pray* together. But do not begin by praying about your problems; just seek the light of God's presence for your darkest night. Even if you are going through "the valley of the shadow of death," know that the promise is sure: The Lord is with you (see Ps. 23:4).

Have you ever thought to pray about your problem instead of complaining? Read again all the things that Paul and Silas did not do. You do not find any meanness or retaliation in their prayer. Can you agree with them to *two-pray* and not complain?

Worship-pray and *praise-pray* are the very best ways to pray, because you focus on God, rather than yourself. When you focus on God, your problems seem to go away until you bring them up again. If you worship God, you can turn any room into a sanctuary. God will come to hear your praises. So bring Him into your darkest night by worshiping Him.

WHAT UNBELIEF DOES TO YOUR PRAYER

1. You lack persistence (see Matt. 7:7).
2. You doubt (see Heb. 11:6).
3. You have unknown sin (see John 9:31).
4. You harbor unconfessed sin (see Isa. 59:1-2).
5. You are selfish (see Jas. 4:2-3).
6. You don't ask (see Jas. 4:2).

Watch for ministry opportunities that come when you *two-pray* yourself through problems. Just as the infant church in Philippi was strengthened because of a prayer meeting in jail, so you can strengthen your ministry when you *two-pray* in times of darkness and tribulation.

Remember Paul's exhortation to the Philippians years later: "The things which you learned and received and heard and saw in me, these do, and the God of peace will be with you" (Phil. 4:9).

TAKE-AWAY PRAYER PRINCIPLES

1. I should pray when problems and troubles come.
2. I should pray when I cannot sleep.

3. I should not complain about difficulties but pray for God's presence in my life. Then prayer can change me as well as my circumstances.

4. I should accept each day that the Lord gives, rejoicing and being glad in it.

5. I should worship God when troubles come, because worship brings God into my situation.

CHAPTER 7

WHEN YOU
Spirit-Pray

Years ago when I was a college president (not yet 30 years old), I submitted a grant proposal to a foundation in Toronto, Canada, seeking a $50,000 gift. I was shortly to discover that I had asked for the wrong amount of money in the wrong way and that my proposal had not been written on the correct forms. I did everything wrong—but I had one thing working in my favor: I was energetic. The president of the foundation granted me an interview because I had written a letter requesting it, and before he could answer, I followed up with a phone call. He liked my enthusiasm.

I flew from Winnipeg to Toronto and then took a taxi to the headquarters of one of the largest companies in Canada to meet with him. When I got out of the taxi, he said, "You shouldn't have spent that money on a taxi. I would have come to the airport to pick you up." The president was a devoted Christian and an outstanding businessman. He knew that small, struggling Bible colleges didn't have a lot of money, especially for long taxi rides.

After I made my proposal to the corporation's budget committee, the company president moved to table any action on my request. I was devastated. I had prayed for $50,000, and I felt I had been turned down.

But then the president took me into his office and began explaining. "Your proposal is not written properly: You've asked for funds for a spiritual project that we can't support because we are a secular company; and you've asked for the wrong amount of money." Then he said, "Let's sit down and rewrite your proposal."

We sat at a large conference table in his office and rewrote the proposal, using the correct form. I changed the project from rebuilding our chapel to rebuilding classrooms and only asked for $25,000, because the president told me that this was the maximum amount of their grants. At the next meeting of the budget committee, our proposal passed; we eventually received a check for $25,000.

While I was praying for money, God answered my prayer by giving me the help of the corporation's president. God used the president's wisdom and position to answer my prayer.

In the same way, the Holy Spirit helps you when you pray the wrong way or you ask for the wrong thing. At such times the Holy Spirit is right beside you, redirecting your prayers to God because your Father knows what you need before you ask (see Matt. 6:8).

When unconfessed sin in your life blocks your prayers, the Holy Spirit shines the light of conviction to show you what to confess. When you don't know the right thing to pray for, the Holy Spirit places a burden upon your heart to pray for the right things, things you hadn't even thought about before. All of this is the Holy Spirit helping you—and usually you don't even realize it.

Likewise the Spirit also helps in our weaknesses. For we do not know what we should pray for as we ought, but the Spirit Himself makes intercession for us with groanings which cannot be uttered. Now He who searches the hearts knows what the mind of the Spirit is, because He makes intercession for the saints according to the will of God (Rom. 8:26-27).

PRAYER AND THE HELP OF THE SPIRIT

The Mystery of the Spirit's Aid
In our limited human wisdom we do not always know what to pray for; but the Holy Spirit anticipates what we need. The word "likewise" in Romans 8:26 refers back to the preceding verses that describe glorious expectations to be revealed at the second coming of Jesus Christ. Just as we don't understand when and how God is going to transform the present world by this event, "likewise" we don't understand when, where and how the Holy Spirit helps us pray.

Who Is the Spirit?
Who is this that the above Scripture says "helps in our weaknesses"? Later in the verse Paul identifies Him as "the Spirit Himself," indicating that he is referring to the Holy Spirit, the third Person of the Trinity. Three times in the passage He is simply called "the Spirit" because that is His primary name. The Scriptures call Him the Holy Spirit fewer than 100 times, but He is called "the Spirit" more than 400 times. The term "holy" describes the Spirit's pure nature that is separate from any type of sin.

Why Does the Spirit Pray for You?
We need the Spirit to pray for us because we are sinners who cannot come into the presence of a holy God alone. So the Holy Spirit comes alongside to "partner" with us so we can come into God's presence. Because the Spirit is the *Holy* Spirit, He brings you directly in to the presence of the Holy Father. When you can't get in, He gets you in.

Remember how the president of that corporation got me into the budget meeting because he liked me and wanted to do something for Winnipeg Bible College? Just as he got me "in" with the budget committee, the Holy Spirit gets you in to the presence of God.

In fact, the work of the Spirit is so important as you *Spirit-pray* that here's a checklist to help you be sure that you are in tune with what He wants to do in your life.

Holy Spirit Checklist
Are you indwelt by the Spirit (He comes in at salvation)?
Are you baptized by the Spirit (placed into Jesus)?
Are you filled by the Spirit (yielded to Him)?
Are you seeking the Holy Spirit's guidance?
Are you walking in the Spirit?
Have you confessed all known sins?
Are you studying to learn more of the Spirit?
Are you faithfully using your spiritual gifts?
Should you apologize to someone you've offended?
Are you worshiping God biblically?

How Does the Holy Spirit Help?

Many times you don't know what to pray for, because you are limited by the flesh. But the Holy Spirit knows, and He will help make intercession for you. Why would He do that? Because Jesus asked the Father to send the Holy Spirit to help you. "I will pray the Father, and He will give you another helper, that He may abide with you forever" (John 14:16).

Jesus called the Holy Spirit a "helper," which is perhaps Jesus' favorite term for the Spirit, because He knows that the Holy Spirit will help you in many ways, including helping you in prayer. (See my book *The Names of the Holy Spirit*, chapter 1 in particular.) The Bible teaches that the Spirit helps us pray in several ways:

He reminds us what to pray (see John 14:26).
He motivates us when to pray (see John 14:27).
He guides us in our prayers (see John 16:13).
He will point us to Jesus (see John 15:26).
He gives us strength to pray (see Col. 1:8-12).

Help with Your Primary Weakness

Back to Romans 8:26, Paul says that the Spirit also helps us in our weakness. What is your greatest weakness? The *King James Version* uses the word "infirmities." In the original language, the word is actually in the singular, meaning your one weakness or your greatest weakness. Most people's greatest weakness is unbelief; the Holy Spirit will help you with that primary infirmity. We don't pray more boldly because of unbelief. We don't pray persistently because of unbelief. We don't pray for big things because of unbelief.

Because the Holy Spirit is God, He knows what you need, He knows how to get it, and He knows when it will come about. There is no unbelief with the Holy Spirit; you are the unbeliever. When the Holy Spirit helps your "infirmities," He is helping you overcome unbelief to get answers to prayer.

WHY THE SPIRIT'S PRAYERS ARE EFFECTIVE

1. He knows our motives in asking; He searches the heart.
2. He knows the mind of God; He knows how to ask.
3. He knows the will of God; He knows what God wants to give us.
4. He knows the heart of God; He knows how God feels toward us.

Why Is Prayer Not More "Natural"?

Some people would say that prayer is extremely natural, because when people get into a tight spot, they yell out, "Help me, God!" Some have even said that when a person uses God's name to curse, they are subconsciously asking for God. Not so! That's using His name out of fear or anger. When the Bible says, "We do not know what we should pray for as we ought" (Rom. 8:26, *KJV*), it means that our unbelief keeps us from truly praying. When you *truly* pray, you put all confidence in God to answer your request. You stop trusting yourself, which is the tendency of the "natural" man, and you trust God instead.

But to put all your trust in God and not self, without the gift of grace, is not only hard, but it's also impossible. Since "faith" is a gift of God, the Holy Spirit must come alongside you to help you believe or trust God for answers.

Some people don't understand this tension. The old adage is "Praise the Lord, and pass the ammunition." This implies that believing prayer isn't enough; you must also work to get your prayer answered. Such an idea also suggests that prayer requires self-effort. As a result, some will trust themselves, their money, human wisdom—anything but God, because if they totally trusted in God, it would cost them a lot in repentance. You can't trust God and live a sinful, selfish life.

The "natural man" thinks he knows everything; but this passage says "We do not know what to pray for." "Know" is from the Greek *oida,* which means "intuitive knowledge." People do not have innate knowledge about God. They need the Holy Spirit to tell them what to pray and to actually help them pray.

Have you ever *two-prayed* with the Holy Spirit? Why not try it now?

How Does the Spirit Intercede for Us?

Romans 8:26 also says that the Spirit "makes intercession for us." What does this mean? An intercessor is one who speaks for, or on behalf of, another person. When you don't know what to say to God, the Holy Spirit becomes your intercessor. Sometimes you may feel that you don't even know what you need; but the Spirit knows, and He tells God what you need. We have many intercessors who speak for us:

Who Intercedes for You?
1. In legal matters: a lawyer
2. In sports matters: an agent
3. With problems on the job: a union steward
4. When purchasing a house: a realtor
5. In religious requests: the Holy Spirit

Since you trust intercessors to speak for you in the natural world, why can't you trust the Holy Spirit to be your Intercessor in the spiritual world?

How Does the Spirit Pray with "Groanings"?

What does it mean when Romans 8:26 says that the Spirit's intercession is "with groanings which cannot be uttered"? No matter how deeply you look into your heart, you never get to the bottom of it. Even though you are desperate for God, in your heart you usually hang on to something from this world. So when you never get absolutely honest with God, what does the Holy Spirit do? He "makes intercession for us with groanings."

The word for "groanings" means "strong desires." It is similar to "begging with tears." The Holy Spirit holds back nothing when He begs for the things that you need. Jeremiah 17:9 says that "the heart is deceitful above all things." But even when you can't be entirely honest or utter the truth from the bottom of your heart, isn't it good to know that the Holy Spirit can pray these unutterable things with "strong desire"?

Can You Hear the Holy Spirit Praying?

Sometimes when a spouse or parent is in the other room talking on the phone, you accidentally lift up an extension and hear part of the conversation. If you could listen in on the Holy Spirit praying for you, could you understand His words? No! The Holy Spirit prays "with groanings which cannot be uttered." This means that we cannot understand the meaning of the words He is using.

This is not an issue of speaking in tongues or charismatic language. Listen to the kinds of groanings that occur in our everyday life. A halfback may groan as he crashes into the line with every ounce of energy in his body. It is his strong desire to make a fourth down, or even a touchdown. Listen to a woman groaning in childbirth, straining every muscle of her body; she does it to give birth to a child.

Likewise, when you are praying with strong desire but lack the words to express it, the Holy Spirit will pray for you with such strong groanings that you can't understand it. But the Father who hears the Holy Spirit understands the groanings, and He will answer your prayer.

The Power of *Spirit-Pray*

When you get discouraged in prayer, remember that the Holy Spirit is your prayer partner. In Him you have a strong partner who will not give up.

Think of a little child over her head in a swimming pool, struggling to get to shallow water. Her father comes along to help her, because he loves her. He makes sure she swims out of trouble. In the same way when you struggle with prayer, let the Holy Spirit become your partner. Even in prayer, your power is human. But you can depend on the divine power of the Spirit to get your prayers through to God.

HOW TO BE FILLED WITH THE SPIRIT

1. You must want the Spirit.
2. You must repent of your sin.
3. You must ask God's forgiveness.
4. You must sincerely ask the Spirit to come in.
5. You must believe the Spirit will come in.
6. You must act upon the Spirit's presence.

How Dependable Is the Spirit's Work?

The Spirit's intercessory work is mentioned twice in Romans 8:26-27. In verse 26 the construction of the original language implies the *process* of interceding. This is what the Holy Spirit does when He joins with us in prayer. As we are praying, He joins with us in the process.

In verse 27 the word construction implies the *position* of interceding. In His position as the third Person in the Trinity, the Holy

Spirit makes sure our prayers get through. You can't lose when you *two-pray* with the Holy Spirit. He knows how to make sure that your prayers get all the way to the Father. Why? Because He knows how to present your request to the Father (the process), and He's right there by the Father (i.e., has the position to do so, since He is the third Person of the Trinity).

The Spirit and Unanswered Prayer

Many people have prayed, but they don't get an answer. Maybe you identify with them because you don't get your prayers answered. Why? The answer may be that you are not in a right relationship to the Holy Spirit. Your mouth may say "Lord, I need you," but your actions say "Lord, don't mess in my life."

To live in right relationship with the Spirit requires being filled with the Spirit. That's what it takes for Him to work with you in intercession. So get filled with the Spirit, and get your prayers answered.

When you are filled with the Holy Spirit, He will partner with you in prayer. Because He is holy, He will make you holy. Because He is the Spirit, He will make you spiritual.

YOUR TURN NOW

The Holy Spirit has prayed with you on many occasions, but you didn't even know it. You received answers to prayer, but never realized the Holy Spirit was partnering with you. Now you know! Think how much better you can pray because you realize the Holy Spirit will come alongside to help your prayers get through.

Perhaps you need to learn to *two-pray* with the Holy Spirit, as in the following prayer:

> Lord, I come to You with the Holy Spirit, and we both agree that I want to be spiritual. We both agree that I want cleansing from sin. We both agree I want Your power in my life. We both agree that we need an answer to prayer.

Now that you realize the Holy Spirit will *two-pray* with you, you should have more faith to ask for greater things, more boldness to ask for the impossible and more wisdom to ask for the things God wants you to have.

TAKE-AWAY PRAYER PRINCIPLES

1. I can be more effective in *two-pray* with the Holy Spirit.
2. I can pray even when my faith falters, because the Holy Spirit helps my unbelief.
3. I can be holy because His holiness makes me holy; I can be spiritual because His spirituality makes me spiritual.
4. I can be effective even when I don't know what to pray, when to pray and how to pray, because the Holy Spirit helps me.
5. I can *two-pray* with the Holy Spirit, because He helps me in the process and because of His position in the Trinity.
6. Even though I cannot probe my heart's depths, the groanings of the Holy Spirit assure me of integrity.

Look through God's eyes.
If we recognize this power,   11/20/02
our struggles become nothing.

The things unseen are eternal.

CHAPTER 8

WHEN YOU
Jesus-Pray

I love to hear Jack Hayford pray because he prays with Jesus. Even though I am not a member of his church, I usually view his worship service on television each Sunday night when I return home from my church. Why? Because I feel I am in the presence of God when he prays.

Once I heard Jack pray, "Lord, I agree with You that You want this brother healed," and he prayed for the healing of a person in his church. On another occasion he prayed, "Lord, I agree with You that none should perish, so I pray for the salvation of ____."

Wow! I thought, *Jack is an effective intercessor because he agrees with Jesus in prayer!*

When Jack Hayford introduced to me to the concept of praying with Jesus, he changed my attitude toward Jesus in prayer. I had always known that Jesus was my intercessor in heaven and that as He was making intercession at the right hand of God the Father, He was praying *for* me (see Rom. 8:34). Now I realize that Jesus will join *with* me in making intercession for my requests—if I invite Him. As the author of the book of Hebrews wrote:

But He [Jesus], because He continues forever, has an unchangeable priesthood. Therefore He is also able to save to the uttermost those who come to God through Him, since He always lives to make intercession for them (Heb. 7:24-25).

TWO-PRAYING WITH JESUS

Perhaps you don't have anyone who can pray with you, so *two-praying* with a prayer partner is not an option. But everyone can *two-pray* with Jesus. I call this *Jesus-pray*. This chapter can revolutionize your prayer ministry, if you will learn to pray with Him. Let's look at the basis of this intercessory role of Jesus that enables Him to partner with you in prayer.

In Heaven As It Was on Earth

Jesus prays now in heaven because He had the habit of praying often on Earth. When you look at the earthly life of Jesus, He was busy preaching, talking to people, healing the sick and doing other signs and miracles that evidenced His great compassion. But beyond these, don't forget the many times Jesus was found praying.

Even the night before He faced death, Jesus spent the darkest hours praying. "Then they came to a place which was named Gethsemane; and He said to His disciples, 'Sit here while I pray'" (Mark 14:32). Looking at other instances in Scripture teaches us several important things from Jesus' prayer life.

1. *His example.* "Teach us to pray" (Luke 11:1).
2. *His petition.* "Glorify Me together with Yourself" (John 17:5).
3. *His spiritual warfare.* "Keep them from the evil one" (John 17:15).
4. *His evangelism by prayer.* "I . . . pray . . . for those who will believe in Me" (John 17:20).
5. *His forgiveness.* "Father, forgive them" (Luke 23:34).

Jesus Prays As a Sinless High Priest

Even when facing the most severe temptations (see Matt. 4:1-10), Jesus did not sin. When you read the book of Hebrews, you realize that one of Jesus' qualifications to be your intercessor is the fact that He lived a sinless life. "For such a High Priest was fitting for us, who is holy, harmless, undefiled, separate from sinners, and has become higher than the heavens" (Heb. 7:26).

Jesus' Humanity Means He Understands Your Needs

On Earth, Jesus was the God-Man, meaning He was completely God at all times while being completely Man at all times. My pastor has often said, "Jesus could not be more God than He was in eternity, He could not be more Man than He was on Earth." Because He lived on Earth in a physical body, He identifies with all your needs in the body. He did not give up His human qualities when He returned to heaven! He understands your physical problems and predicaments, so He can pray all the more sympathetically for you. "But this *man*, because he continueth ever, hath an unchangeable priesthood" (Heb. 7:24, *KJV*, emphasis added).

WHY JESUS CAN BE YOUR INTERCESSOR

1. He is holy, embodying the nature of God.
2. He is harmless, never hurting anyone.
3. He is undefiled, having faced problems like yours without sinning.
4. He is separate from the world, never giving in to temptation.

This "unchangeable priesthood" means that just because Jesus has gone back to heaven doesn't mean that His intercession has changed or ceased. He prays for you in temptation, just as He did when He told Peter, "Satan has asked for you, that he may sift you as wheat. But I have prayed for you, that your faith should not fail" (Luke 22:31-32). Jesus also promises that He will never allow us to be tempted beyond what we can bear (see 1 Cor. 10:13).

So the next time you are tempted to sin, stop and pray, "Lord, I agree with You that I should be victorious over sin."

Jesus Will Separate You from the World

What is the main concern of Christian parents for their teenager? That God will keep their children from the influence of the world, the flesh and the devil. In the same way, Jesus' intercession for you in heaven is to protect you from sin on Earth, to make you godly, to separate you from the world.

Jesus "is also able to save to the uttermost those who come to God through Him, since He always lives to make intercession for them" (Heb. 7:25). The word "uttermost" means "completely." When you are saved to the uttermost, you are separated to the uttermost from the world.

The Power Is in the Blood

What is the basis of Jesus' intercession for you? He does not just ask for the Father to answer Him because He understands your problems, nor is it that He desires to use you in His service. Jesus sits at the right hand of the Father interceding for you on the basis of His shed blood to forgive your sins. He "does not need daily, as those high priests, to offer up sacrifices . . . for this He did once for all when He offered up Himself" (Heb. 7:27).

You must realize the truth of the old song "There's Power in the Blood." When Jesus prays for you, He is pleading on the basis of the power in His blood to forgive your sins and to make you godly.

HOW YOU CAN PRAY WITH JESUS

Just because you have the privilege of *two-praying* with Jesus does not mean that you turn all the praying over to Him. You must be prepared to actively participate in this prayer partnership in several ways.

Remember the Blood

You must come into the presence of God just like the Israelites came into the Tabernacle. There was only one way into the Tabernacle—at the place where blood sacrifices were made on the brazen altar. It is still true today that "without shedding of blood there is no remission [of sins]" (Heb. 9:22).

THE BASIS OF JESUS' INTERCESSION FOR YOU

1. He is interceding to keep you from sin.
2. He is interceding for you to live for God to the uttermost.
3. He is reminding the Father that His blood covers your sins.

When I pray by myself or with friends, most of the time I begin, "Lord, I have sinned. I come to You through the blood of Jesus Christ. Please forgive my sins, for I have fallen short of doing the right thing. Forgive the sins that I commit ignorantly and those I do with my eyes wide open."

Someone chatting with me years ago told me he didn't like the way I began praying. He suggested that I sounded like I was the "prodigal son" coming back to God and that I might cause people to think I had some great hidden sin. I thanked my friend for his concern, but reminded him that even the apostle Paul referred to himself as the chief of sinners (see 1 Tim. 1:15). When he wrote this in his old age, Paul was probably closer to the Lord than at any other time; yet he realized his sinfulness. I think the closer you get to God, the more you see your imperfections, just like the more light you shine on the kitchen, the more places that need cleaning.

Plan for Moment-by-Moment Cleansing

Not only must we enter the Tabernacle—God's presence—through the blood sacrifice, we must walk daily depending upon the blood to cleanse every sin. "If we walk in the light as He is in the light, we have fellowship with one another, and the blood of Jesus Christ His Son cleanses us from all sin" (1 John 1:7).

To "walk in the light" means to attempt to obey every Scripture and to live as close to the Lord as possible. Even then, however, you need the blood that cleanses from all sin. And the original language here indicates that Christ's blood continually provides moment-by-moment cleansing.

So when you get ready to *two-pray*, you must get rid of any barrier to your fellowship with God. You may have confessed every sin yesterday, but as you walk the dusty roads of life, your feet get dirty. You're not dirty all over, but you may have committed sins of ignorance or omission. Confess these to Jesus, your intercessor. Before you attempt to *two-pray* with a prayer partner on Earth, *Jesus-pray* with your partner in heaven.

Pray Boldly Because Your Sins Are Forgiven

Sometimes your sin makes you fearful in God's presence, taking away your confidence in prayer. You are like the little boy who sneaked into the kitchen and was afraid to ask Mom for a cookie because he tracked his dirty feet across the clean floor. But when the little boy says "I'm sorry" and has his mom's full forgiveness, he can confidently ask for the cookie. In the same way, you can pray boldly when you know your sins are forgiven.

Remember that you are one with your Intercessor. Speaking to His followers, Jesus said, "You [are] in Me, and I in you" (John 14:20). This means you can come boldly to the Father in prayer. As another little boy said, "Jesus has got me covered." You don't have to worry about being imperfect, or that He will throw a past sin in your face. *Two-pray* boldly.

You Depend on the Perfection of Jesus

God expects His children to be perfect, just like you expect your children to behave themselves all the time. When a mother says, "Have a good time, but don't get into trouble," she expects her child to do everything right. But Mother was a kid once; she knows that

TO PRAY IN JESUS' NAME MEANS

You come through the Cross and His blood that cleanses you.
You come through His indwelling life in you.
You come through His intercession at the right hand of the Father.

children "push the envelope." If a child comes back from a date having done something wrong, they try to sneak into the house quickly and jump into bed before Mother can talk with them. Why? They don't want to face Mother.

In the same way, it is sometimes difficult to enter God's presence when you know you are not perfect. If you are too guilty to enter God's presence, there is good news. You can enter His presence in the perfection of his Son. During His days on Earth, Jesus said, "I always do those things that please [the Father]" (John 8:29). And today Jesus stands at the right hand of the Father, still pleasing the Father. Jesus already is in the presence of the Father, and you can be there too in Jesus.

So what should you do? Don't just rejoice in the forgiveness of sins—appropriate your position in Christ. Enter the Father's presence through the perfection of Jesus Christ. Now you can *two-pray* because you stand there before the Father clothed in the righteousness of the Son. "He made Him who knew no sin to be sin for us, that we might become the righteousness of God in Him" (2 Cor. 5:21).

You Won't Get Lost in the Crowd!

If there are over 6 billion people in the world, how could Jesus make intercession for all of them, all the time? Because Jesus is God, who has no limits, He knows everything, He is everywhere present at all times and He can do all things. So He can make intercession for all people, all the time, and the Father will hear every prayer He makes in intercession.

Therefore, when you come to the Father with Jesus to get answers to prayers, you won't get lost in the crowd. When the Father looks around to find you, just as a parent might frantically search for a lost child in a Christmas crowd, don't panic. He knows where you are. He will find you "in Jesus" as the Savior intercedes for you.

Praying in Jesus' Name

You have a wide-open door available to you because Jesus assures us that "Whatever you ask in My name, that I will do" (John 14:13). Because of this assurance, most Christians throughout the centuries have ended their prayers, "in Jesus' name."

I have a friend who always *begins* his prayer, "I come in Jesus' name." Maybe he wants to make sure he gets the Father's attention immediately by starting out with the name of Jesus. Whether you use His name first or last, remember that when you pray in Jesus' name it is not a magical formula that gets you into heaven. Prayer is never automatic—it is personal, intense, face-to-face and based on your relationship with Jesus Christ. When you pray in Jesus' name, you are praying in the person of Jesus and by His authority.

When Jesus told us to ask in His name, His emphasis was not on a formula that includes using His name but on your need to come to the Father through His blood. You come to the Father through Christ's indwelling presence: "I am crucified with Christ: nevertheless I live; yet not I, but Christ liveth in me" (Gal. 2:20, *KJV*). And you come to the Father by entering through Jesus who is your intercessor.

YOUR TURN NOW

Now you can get right through to the Father in prayer because Jesus your intercessor is at the right hand of the Father, making intercession for you. So join Jesus in *two-pray*. It's a wonderful feeling to know the Father won't turn you down when you *Jesus-pray*.

Do you know how to *Jesus-pray*? Or have you experienced it yet? First, you must meet all the conditions of prayer, i.e., do everything required to get answers to your prayers. Second, you must boldly come to the Father in the person of Jesus. If you have sinned, and because you have sinned, He will forgive you because He makes intercession for you on the basis of His blood. When you get close to the Father, make your request in Jesus' name.

Maybe you are not receiving answers to your prayers. The problem is not with Jesus. When you pray "in Jesus," your prayers always get through. Maybe you don't get answers because you are not rightly related to Him. If so, now is the time to take this "spiritual checkup."

Spiritual Checkup
1. Do I know that I am a sinner? (See Rom. 3:23.)
2. Do I realize that my sins will send me to hell? (See Rom. 6:23.)
3. Have I accepted Jesus into my life as Savior? (See John 1:12.)
4. Have I confessed Jesus before others? (See Rom. 10:9.)
5. Am I walking daily in Jesus? (See Col. 2:6.)
6. Have I confessed my sins daily? (See 1 John 1:8-9.)
7. Have I taken up His cross? (See Luke 9:23.)

TAKE-AWAY PRAYER PRINCIPLES

1. I can pray more effectively because Jesus' blood cleanses me.
2. I can *Jesus-pray* because His blood cleanses me, because He indwells me and because He is my intercessor.
3. I have a Savior who understands my needs.
4. I will become more effective in prayer through *Jesus-pray* with Him.

CHAPTER 9

VITAL QUESTIONS AND ANSWERS ABOUT PRAYER PARTNERS

Bill Klassen walked into the office of his pastor, John Maxwell, shortly after the young minister was first called to Skyline Wesleyan Church in San Diego, California. Klassen told Maxwell, "God has called me to pray for you." Out of that interview has grown a 20-year journey in ministry together. Bill Klassen has journeyed on his knees in intercession for John Maxwell, while Maxwell has built the church from 800 to over 3,000 in attendance. At the same time he has built a worldwide leadership ministry called The INJOY Group that has added value to the leadership of hundreds of thousands of people.

This remarkable prayer partnership prompts several questions:

1. How can you know whom to ask to be your prayer partner?
2. How can you know if you are called to be an intercessor?
3. How can you ask someone to be your intercessor?

Pastors and Prayer Partners

Someone could ask, "Could John Maxwell have built his ministry without the prayer support of Bill Klassen?" My answer is that if God had not led Bill to pray for John, He would have sent someone else to intercede for Maxwell as a young pastor.

It also could have been asked, "Would Bill Klassen have had a fruitful prayer ministry without John Maxwell?" My answer is that if God had not directed Bill to pray for John, He would have directed him to someone else. However, in God's plan and purpose, the Lord joined these two men in ministry—a wonderful intercessor and a gifted man of God.

Perhaps you are a potential intercessor who is looking to partner with someone in prayer. Perhaps you want to be an intercessor for another but don't know what to do. Perhaps you need to hear Paul's words to Timothy: "Stir up the gift of God which is in you" (2 Tim. 1:6). If you have an intercessor's ability, it needs to be fanned into a warming fire, so that God's work will go forward.

Or maybe you are a pastor who needs an intercessor. Perhaps someone in your congregation would respond to this need and pray with you or for you. You need to find your intercessor and develop a prayer relationship with him or her.

The answers to the questions above could transform your life and your ministry. First, if you are a minister and you don't have someone interceding for you—as Aaron and Hur held up the arms of Moses—then you can be personally defeated and your ministry might not be as effective as it could be. Second, if you are a layperson, you may have the ability to become a great intercessor for God but miss your primary ministry of intercession, because you don't know how to start looking for a prayer partner. Therefore, let him that has eyes to read, understand (see Matt. 13:13-15).

How to Find a Prayer Partner

God used C. Peter Wagner's book *Prayer Shield* to help me find prayer partners. Since the book told about people who had become his prayer partners, I let it guide me to find my intercessors. I had previously read how R. A. Torrey interceded for Dwight L. Moody and J. Edwin Orr interceded for Billy Graham. I know that when God greatly used a person, He also raised up great prayer warriors for that person. I also want to be used of God, so I wanted someone to pray for me.

My in-laws, Mr. and Mrs. E. B. Forbes, were my greatest prayer support. Every morning after breakfast they had knelt by a couch and interceded for me. Besides giving me my wife, Ruth, their greatest contribution to my ministry was daily prayer for specific needs. When they died, I didn't know how to find replacements for them. I needed prayer warriors.

I read portions of *Prayer Shield* at our church's early Sunday morning prayer meeting, when members of my Bible class gather to pray for each other's needs. When it came time for me to bring my petition forward, I asked them to pray about whether God might be leading one of them to be my prayer partner. Out of that request, Buddy Bryant, a logger and a godly man, became my primary prayer partner.

Here are some suggestions to help you find your own Buddy Bryant.

Look for the Most Obvious Person

When you are looking for a prayer partner, look for the person that you would obviously recognize as a fitting prayer partner. If you are married, your prayer partner should be your mate. The apostle Peter said that husbands should dwell with their wives "with understanding . . . as being heirs together of the grace of life, that your prayers may not be hindered" (1 Pet. 3:7).

If you lead a church or ministry, look to the board that oversees your organization. Perhaps it might be a close friend, or, as in my case, it might be someone who knows you and your ministry well and will pray regularly for you.

Ask God to Give You a Prayer Partner

If you are looking for a prayer partner, the most obvious thing you should do is pray for God to give you one. Ask God for someone (*a*) who has a burden for you and your ministry, so that they will invest time and energy interceding for you; (*b*) who knows how to intercede; and (*c*) who is called to a ministry of interceding.

Be Reciprocal—Pray for Them

Writing to the Thessalonians, Paul asked for reciprocal prayer. First he told them that he was mentioning them in his own prayers (see 1 Thess. 1:2). Then he made the specific request, "Brethren, pray for us" (5:25). Therefore, it would seem that a person who is already praying for others is the person who can recruit prayer partners. While this verse has a general interpretation, it can be applied to you and your prayer partners. The famous "Do unto others as you would have them do unto you" passage can be phrased for this need: "Pray for others as you would have them pray for you."

Pray with Fellow Ministers

One of the most obvious prayer partners for Sunday School teachers is the coteacher of the class. You should pray with those who minister with you. It would be very easy for the two of you to agree together for the Lord's blessing in your ministry. Whether these are full-time or voluntary workers, it should be very easy for you to agree and *two-pray* together with those who minister with you.

Has God Put Someone on Your Heart?

Earlier in this chapter I told of asking the members of an early morning prayer meeting to pray about becoming my prayer partner. I asked them because God had put it upon my heart. I began by telling them, "This book by C. Peter Wagner, *Prayer Shield*, is the greatest book I've ever read for getting people to pray for leaders." I proceeded to read to them from the chapters "Receiving Personal Intercession" and "Maintaining Your Intercessors." Then I asked them to pray for a week to discern whether God was calling one of them to be my intercessor.

The following Sunday, one of the members of the class, Buddy Bryant, said that he would like to be my personal intercessor, i.e., to pray for me every day. Buddy works in the woods each day cutting timber, loading it on logging trucks and driving it to the mill. He explained that the sound of a chainsaw didn't give him much opportunity to talk on the job. He said, "My thoughts are my own, and that's when I spend time in prayer." So each day I have a prayer partner in the woods praying for me and my ministry.

Share the Burden of Your Heart

If people are going to be your prayer partners, you must open up your life to them and share your dreams, plans and problems. They must get very close to your heart. Then the two of you can agree together to claim what Jesus has promised, and it will be done for you by His Father in heaven (see Matt. 18:19).

Share Prayer Requests Frequently

What good are prayer partners if you don't share with them your challenges so they can pray with you? You must have contact with them on a regular basis and share with them different requests from your life and ministry. It is probably best to meet with them on a weekly basis—or more often—so they can be up-to-date in their prayer requests. And beyond just giving them your prayer requests, you will want to share answers to prayer with your prayer partner. If all they do is intercede and never hear what God is doing, they may eventually become discouraged.

In the late 1980s and early 1990s, Liberty University had a $52 million indebtedness, and every month it seemed that the school faced another financial crisis. When it seemed impossible to keep the doors open, Buddy Bryant and I prayed for God to give the university $52 million. We prayed weekly with others for that money in an early Sunday morning prayer meeting. We knew that God was going to answer; it was just a question of how and when.

Finally, Jerry Falwell, Liberty's chancellor, fasted and prayed for 40 days; but God didn't give him the money to save the university. As I related earlier, God told Falwell to "find My heart, not My pocketbook." Our early Sunday morning prayer group kept praying after Falwell ended his 40-day fast. Twenty-five days later, God told Falwell he could now ask for money. He went on a second 40-day fast—eating only 25 days out of 105. At the end of this second fast, God touched one man's heart to give the university $52 million.

I constantly remind the early morning prayer group and Buddy Bryant that God heard their prayers to save the school. That great answer to prayer motivates us to ask for greater things.

Different Partners for Different Challenges

You may choose a different prayer partner for various issues, depending on the subject of concern or burden. A friend may share a prayer burden as a business partner, so the two of you *two-pray* for your business. A wife or husband may be your closest prayer partner for family needs, and you may *two-pray* with a coworker at church for church needs. When you are looking for a prayer partner, God may lead you to more than one. You may have different prayer partners for different areas of your life.

ARE YOU AN INTERCESSOR?

In order to find out if intercession should be your main ministry, ask yourself the following questions. The way you answer these questions will help determine if God is leading you into an intercessory ministry. Some of the questions probe deeply into your heart, and your answers must be honest. When you know the answers to these questions, you will be in a better position to determine if intercessory prayer is your primary calling.

Have Others Been Blessed by Your Prayers?

If you can point to people you have helped through your prayer, if you know that their problems have been solved through your prayer and if you can point to God's intervention through your prayer, then you probably have the gift of intercession.

Do You Have a Burden to Pray for Others?

Many people spend long hours in prayer, but most only pray for themselves, their family and their needs. They don't have a great burden to pray for others. And of course, there is nothing wrong with praying for yourself and your ministry. The Bible teaches us to do that; but the person who has been given the ministry of intercession will have a burden to intercede for other people.

Is Your Greatest Passion to Pray for Others?

God has given us all a ministry, and we should fulfill it faithfully. If you have a ministry of teaching, evangelism, helping or counseling, you will have a great zeal to be used in that ministry. The previous section dealt with the burdens of prayer that may weigh heavy on you. If you have this burden, then intercession is what you must do.

PRAYER PARTNERS MAKE YOUR MINISTRY THEIR MINISTRY

This question, however, deals with your *passion*—what you want to do more than anything else in life? Passion is what gets you up every morning and drives you through the day. Do you love to pray? If your main joy is praying for the ministry of others, then God is probably giving you an intercessory prayer ministry.

Do You Find Joy in Praying for Others?

Some people don't know what really makes them happy. All they know is that they rejoice in some things, and in other things they are disappointed. Do you find great spiritual satisfaction in praying for others? If there were a "spiritual satisfaction meter" attached to your heart, where would intercessory prayer register?

Some people think it is "carnal" to enjoy any aspect of ministry. They think that serving the Lord is like taking castor oil: If it tastes bad, then it must be good. But that is not the teaching of Scripture. Just as I enjoy my ministry of teaching, and my pastor enjoys his ministry of preaching, so you can enjoy a ministry of intercession. So ask yourself a blunt question: "Do I like to pray?"

Some have developed a false humility, thinking that it's egotistical to enjoy what they do in the Lord's work. When someone thanks you for praying for them, it is false humility to say "I didn't do anything." In fact, you did agonize in prayer for that answer. False humility may be a backhanded way for taking credit for something because you want people to respect your humility. If someone thanks you for an answer to prayer, you should say "Let's thank God together for the answer to prayer."

The point is that if your greatest happiness comes in praying for others, you probably are being led into an intercessory prayer ministry.

Do You Feel God's Leading to Be an Intercessor?

This question is very close to the previous questions about prayer burden, prayer desire and prayer satisfaction, because these are factors we use to determine God's will. But this question deals more specifically with how you feel God is leading you. The Bible says, "It is God who works in you both to will and to do for His good pleasure" (Phil. 2:13). If you feel drawn toward intercession, He is probably leading you into this ministry.

I once asked an intercessor how much time she spent in prayer each day. She answered, "As much time as possible." When I asked another intercessor the same question, I got the answer, "Never enough." These answers might help you know whether you are a prayer intercessor. If you have to force yourself to pray, God may not be leading you to become an intercessor. But if you have to force yourself to leave prayer, God could be calling you into a ministry of intercession.

Have You Prayed in Different Ways?

Those who are led to be intercessors will know how to come to God in many different ways. They know how to begin their prayer with *worship-pray*, magnifying God for who He is and what He has done. Intercessors know that when they worship God, His presence will join them, because "The Father is seeking such to worship Him" (John 4:23).

Intercessors must understand the role of *confession-pray*, as well as the concept of identificational repentance. That is, they must confess their own sins as well as the sins of others around them, as Nehemiah and Daniel confessed the sins of Israel (see Neh. 1:6; Dan. 9:5).

Intercessors must make supplication about the life and ministry of other people. They must move into the realm of petition whereby they ask God for specific answers to prayer in their life.

Intercessors must understand *warfare-pray* whereby they wrestle with the evil one for spiritual protection of leaders, as well as praying for the defeat of demonic powers. They must pray for victory for themselves as well as for those for whom they are interceding.

Many people who come to God think only of worshiping the Lord or asking Him for answers to their needs. While these types of prayer are needed, the one who would be an intercessor must make use of all types of prayer. If you have come to God in many different ways, He may have given you the ministry of intercession.

Do You Seek Answers Persistently?

Intercessors not only love to pray, but they will also pray for long periods of time until they get through to God with their requests. They know how to get answers. Therefore ask yourself, "Am I persistent in seeking answers to prayer?"

You also need to ask, "Am I hearing regularly from God?" If God speaks to you regularly when you are alone with Him in prayer and in the Word, then you may have the gift of intercession. Do you sense God working in your spirit as you intercede? Also, do you sense God teaching you more about prayer? If you are persistent in prayer, perhaps God wants you to be an intercessor.

Do You Get Confirmation from Others?

If God has called you to be a prayer intercessor, others should see
this ministry in your life, especially if you have a prayer partner.
God should show your partner that you have a special ministry of
prayer.

The renowned intercessor for Charles Finney (the evangelist
who introduced the "General Awakening," 1830-1840) was a man
called Father Noah. Another prayer warrior, Graham Fitzpatrick,
spent time interceding for Finney but was unknown and had little
experience in being a prayer partner. He asked God to confirm his
ministry, praying, "Show me if I am to be an intercessor." God
answered that prayer through Father Noah, who came to Graham
Fitzpatrick and confirmed that he was to be an intercessor for
Finney. Later, another man and woman at different times also told
Fitzpatrick that he had the gift of intercessory prayer.

However, some intercessors are completely unknown to the
world, because some prayer warriors do not share with anyone what
they do in their prayer closet. Perhaps they're more effective because
they don't tell anyone. So this question would not apply to them—
and may not apply to you. God can give believers an intercessory
ministry even though no one else recognizes it. But if other people
do recognize the effectiveness of your prayers, then God might be
leading you into a public intercessory prayer ministry.

YOUR TURN NOW

Now you have some ideas about how to find a prayer partner for
your ministry, and how to discover if this is your calling. Review all
the practical suggestions and put them to work. But don't just ask
God; speak with others also. If you're a leader looking for a prayer
partner, learn to share requests with those in your ministry. Tell
them often and tell them with passion why you need prayer. This
is your way of giving to them a burden to pray for you. Don't forget to share answers to your prayer requests. When others pray for
you and then hear how God has answered those prayers, they will

be motivated to pray more for you, perhaps becoming your prayer partners.

And if you're wondering if you have a ministry of intercession, this chapter has given you some hard questions to ask yourself. I didn't make the questions hard to scare you off. Rather, I made them challenging so that when you answer them you'll know for sure whether you have the ministry of intercession.

Now that you have some ideas, put them to work. If God puts a leader on your heart, go to him with your burden. Talk it out. This is the way God will link you up with someone so you can be his or her prayer partner. From that point, God will open up your ministry to greater areas of usefulness.

TAKE-AWAY PRAYER PRINCIPLES

1. I can find someone to be my prayer partner by first asking God and then asking the person God puts upon my heart.
2. I must give myself to those whom God has lead to be my prayer partners.
3. I must share with my faithful prayer partners answers to our prayers.
4. I can find out if my ministry is one of intercession by asking and answering hard questions.
5. I will usually have others tell me if intercession is my main ministry.
6. I must *want* to be an intercessor before I discover if that's the ministry God has for me.

ENDNOTES

Chapter 1

1. Boniface, quoted in Charles Henry Robinson, *The Conversion of Europe* (London, England: Longmans, Green and Co., 1917), p. 378.
2. King Mangs II, quoted in Robinson, *The Conversion of Europe*, p. 378.
3. Dwight L. Moody, quoted in Elmer Towns, *Understanding the Deeper Life* (Old Tappan, NJ: Revell, 1988), pp. 224-225.
4. Bill Bright, "The Four Spiritual Laws," *Campus Crusade for Christ International*, 1995. http://www.crusade.org/fourlaws/ (accessed January 3, 2002).

Chapter 5

1. John Wesley, source unknown.

GLOSSARY

Agree-Pray—Prayer partners coming together in harmony and on the biblical standards for prayer. Jesus promises that this agreement will result in answered prayer (see Matt. 18:19).

Ask-Pray—When you specifically ask for an answer from God.

Bible-Pray—When you quote the Bible as you are praying, so that your requests are biblical.

Clean-Pray—See *Confessing-Pray*.

Communion-Pray—See *Fellowship-Pray*.

Confident-Pray—Praying with a joyful and confident spirit, knowing that God is listening to your request.

Confessing-Pray—When you pray after acknowledging your sins by confessing them, repenting of them and asking God to forgive you. Then you determine to live above those temptations and are spiritually ready to pray.

Continue-Pray—See *Wait-Pray*.

Discipline-Pray—When two believers come together habitually to pray for the right thing in the right way.

Effective-Pray—When you and your prayer partner meet the conditions and pray together, getting the answers you seek.

Evangelistic-Pray—When you pray for the salvation of specific individuals.

Faith-Ask—See *Faith-Pray*.

Faith-Pray—Praying with the firm belief that you will receive the things for which you ask. Often this confidence emerges when one prayer partner encourages the other so that both believe they will receive the things for which they ask.

Fellowship-Pray—When you and your prayer partner join in a oneness of spirit to pray.

Harmony-Pray—See *Fellowship-Pray*.

Hymn-Pray—When two people use hymns to express their prayers.

Insight-Pray—When a prayer partner gains spiritual understanding from the other, or from God, as they pray together.

Intercede-Pray—When you ask God to supply the specific needs of others.

Jesus-Pray—When you agree with Jesus for a prayer request, knowing that He is interceding for you in heaven.

Joy-Pray—When the prayer of one fills the other with spiritual happiness.

Listen-Pray—When you hear the request of the other person and agree with him or her for the answer.

Marriage Harmony-Pray—When husband and wife have marital harmony that influences their joint intercession to God.

Outreach-Pray—When two agree for the salvation of an unsaved person(s), and pray together for their conversion.

Partner-Pray—See *Two-Pray*.

Search-Pray—When two wait before God in prayer, searching for an answer.

Solo-Pray—When you pray by yourself.

Spirit-Pray—When the Holy Spirit "picks you up" in prayer to lift you to a higher spiritual level of intercession.

Success-Pray—See *Effective-Pray*.

Support-Pray—When you want the answer for which you pray but lack sufficient faith, you can agree with your prayer partner because of his or her strong faith.

Two-Pray—When two people who meet God's conditions for having their prayers answered partner in prayer and agree that God will give them an answer. (See also *Jesus-Pray* and *Spirit-Pray*.)

Vision-Pray—When the vision of one prayer partner is communicated to the other so that they are both praying for the same results in a project.

Wait-Pray—When you and another are praying to God but realize that the timing is wrong for an immediate answer.

Warfare-Pray—When prayer partners wrestle with the enemy, i.e., Satan and his demons, against an attack or severe temptation.

Worship-Pray—When the focus of prayer partners is to worship or magnify God in prayer.

ABOUT THE AUTHOR

Elmer L. Towns is dean of the School of Religion at Liberty University in Lynchburg, Virginia, where he teaches the 2,000-member Pastor's Sunday School class at Thomas Road Baptist Church. He is a Gold Medallion Award-winning author whose books include *Fasting for Spiritual Breakthrough* and *Praying the 23rd Psalm*. Elmer Towns and his wife, Ruth, have three grown children.

ALSO BY ELMER TOWNS

The Names of Jesus

My Father's Names

The Names of the Holy Spirit

Fasting for Spiritual Breakthrough

Praying the Lord's Prayer for Spiritual Breakthrough

My Angel Named Herman

Praying the 23rd Psalm

What Every Sunday School Teacher Should Know

MORE OF THE BEST OF ELMER TOWNS!

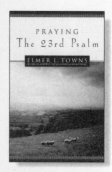